TO LIVE UNTIL WE SAY GOOD-BYE

TO LIVE UNTIL WE SAY GOOD-BYE

Text by

Elisabeth Kübler-Ross

Photographs by

Mal Warshaw

PRENTICE-HALL, INC./Englewood Cliffs, N.J.

To Live Until We Say Good-Bye, Text by Elisabeth Kübler-Ross, M.D.,
Photographs by Mal Warshaw
Copyright © 1978 by Ross Medical Associates, S.C., and Mal Warshaw
All rights reserved. No part of this book may be
reproduced in any form or by any means, except
for the inclusion of brief quotations in a review,
without permission in writing from the publisher.
Printed in the United States of America
Prentice-Hall International, Inc., London
Prentice-Hall of Australia, Pty. Ltd., Sydney
Prentice-Hall of Canada, Ltd., Toronto
Prentice-Hall of India Private Ltd., New Delhi
Prentice-Hall of Japan, Inc., Tokyo
Prentice-Hall of Southeast Asia Pte. Ltd., Singapore
Whitehall Books Limited, Wellington, New Zealand
10   9   8   7   6   5   4   3   2   1

Art Direction and Design by Hal Siegel

Library of Congress Cataloging in Publication Data
Kübler-Ross, Elisabeth.
To live until we say good-bye.
1.   Death—Psychological aspects.   2.   Terminal care.
3.   Terminal care facilities.   4.   Future life.
I.   Warshaw, Mal.   II.   Title.
BF789.D4K83   155.9'37   78-10301
ISBN 0-13-922955-8
ISBN 0-13-922948-5 pbk.

CONTENTS

In addition to the patients in the book—we thank:

Rev. Michael Stolpman, Hospice at Roger's Memorial Hospital, Milwaukee; Sister Cecilia and Sister Mary David of St. Rose's Home, New York; Dennis Rezendes and John Abbott, Hospice, New Haven; Lucy Kroll; The Staff of Shanti Nilaya; Robert Sussman Stewart, Special Projects Editor, Prentice-Hall

PREFACE *by Mal Warshaw*

In a recent six-month period I lost four of the people closest to me—my parents, a cousin and a best friend—and almost lost my wife's mother who hovered between life and death for many months. These events, coming as they did within such an incredibly short period, profoundly affected me and intensified the experience of encountering the end of life.

When Richard Bove, a colleague at Pratt Institute, where I was teaching, suggested during that period that death should be the subject of a photographic book, I was immediately drawn to the idea. My wife, Betty, caught the excitement and saw the value of trying to capture visually the various aspects of the process of dying. It was her encouragement, her intellect, and most important, her generosity in allowing me to share with her her own terror, fears, and fantasies about dying that opened up in me my own deeply buried feelings and started a process of investigation in order to seek answers to our common anxieties about death.

My friend and agent, Lucy Kroll, introduced me to Beth, a vital woman just 42 years old, who was dying of cancer and was willing to share that experience and permit me to photograph the terminal phase of her life.

After I was well into working with Beth and had taken hundreds of photographs of her, a friend suggested that I show them to his friend Elisabeth Kübler-Ross. Dr. Kübler-Ross and I met and talked, and out of that encounter grew an agreement to work together, as well as a friendship, mutual admiration, and respect. Knowing Dr. Kübler-Ross with her special insights and qualities has been one of the most important gifts this collaboration has brought me.

Working with Beth and having recently observed my friends and family in a similar situation, I noted that the faces of people who have a terminal disease, and who have come to terms with their own impending death, have a look that is a marvelous combination of tranquility and incredible power and insight. What I hoped to do was to capture the essence of that look in a photograph, so that those feelings could be broadly shared. And it was evident at the outset that a series of photographs would be necessary to show something of the process and to provide a frame of reference for each individual history.

Usually a photographer enjoys a unique, meaningful relationship with his subject, whether the subject is human, a scene in nature, or an inanimate object. He is an observer, detached from the scene, objective—with a visceral sense of the aesthetics in any given situation. He develops what social workers call a "therapeutic stance" which allows his artistry, professionalism, and expertise to function at maximum levels. Under most circumstances this works.

Any "distancing" from the subjects in this work, however, was unthinkable. Happily for me (and I hope my work) my subjects became my friends. There is no way to remain the slightest bit aloof from a dying friend if you want to keep the channels of communication open and share the experience.

A major challenge in making the photographs for this book was dealing with the unknown. There is no way to predict the exact second when something dramatic or something filled with intense meaning is going to happen. I wanted to be there, standing in the right place, with the right lens, to capture what Robert Frank called "the humanity of the moment." To prearrange this was obviously impossible. A large part of the technique I developed was to invest the time, to be available, to know, to understand, and to be a part of what was happening, to be guided by my instincts, and to let my sense of human connection serve as a focal point.

The luxury of working this way was made possible by the present state of the art of photography. I worked with existing light, used no special lights or popping flashes, so that the camera would intrude as little as possible. All the photographs were taken with 35mm single-reflex cameras. The availability of fast film plus a variety of fast lenses greatly increased my ability to adapt to a great variety of ever changing environments.

There are no posed pictures in this book. I asked my friends to permit me to be present (in the background with my camera) as an observer of the small, incidental events of daily life, as well as, of course, of the special times.

My subjects became very important in my life. They were my teachers. They were making me examine myself in ways I had previously avoided. It was painful, yet strangely reassuring. I found that as I permitted myself to confront the fact of dying, I was more fully embracing life. I felt lighter and more at ease with myself.

I shall always be grateful to our friends for welcoming us into their lives: to Beth, to Louise, to Linda and Jamie, to Jack, and to all the terminal patients for sharing their most precious possession—the short time they had left.

I have tried to record in photographs the various developments in the process of dying, the visual images of the inner struggle to accept the inevitability of death.

I hope that as you read and look at what follows, you too will become more comfortable with the idea of dying and be able to live, as I now do, more freely.

INTRODUCTION
by Elisabeth Kübler-Ross

I first met Mal Warshaw through a mutual friend who was familiar with my work with terminally ill patients and with Mal's search to understand better the mystery of death. After an initial conversation with Mal, during which he shared his interests with me, I invited him to come to my house, where I had an opportunity not only to meet Mal the photographer, but Mal the person, who, like so many other people, cared enough to become involved in a field that too many people try to avoid.

It was clear that Mal, like so many others in our society, was not at peace with the issue of death. But he had one great advantage, and that was the willingness to look at his own fear, guilt, and unfinished business, and try to find answers to the many questions he had, not only about the issue of death and dying, but about life and living itself and the care we give to those who have to face their own finiteness.

Mal had brought with him a stack of pictures of a gallant lady who valiantly fought cancer and finally succumbed to it. With his gifts and talents, his searching mind and his eyes that can see what most people overlook, Mal had grasped aspects of a woman's living and dying in the photographs of his friend Beth; and as we looked at them we started to discuss the many lessons that terminally ill people are able to give us: not only in their increased wisdom and depth, in the communication that they are able to develop with us during the course of a terminal illness, but also in their facial expressions and their willingness to have pictures taken of them which, we hope, will reach many people and prove to the skeptics that dying is an important part of life.

It is in these pictures that they say, in a memorable symbolic language, what it is like to go through the struggle, through the pain, through the loneliness, and, like a rough rock that is put in a tumbler, end up a piece of jewelry. Those facing a terminal, devastating illness, and having the courage to accept it, to say yes to it, will emerge from the struggle with the radiance of a jewel which, as so remarkably demonstrated through Mal's photography, can be seen in their outward expression.

So it is the purpose of this book to show what can and will happen to human beings, young and old, child and adult alike, when they are in the process of being destroyed by a malignant growth and yet can emerge as a butterfly emerges from a cocoon with a sense of peace and freedom, not only in themselves, but in those who are willing to share their final moments and who have the courage to say good-bye, knowing that every good-bye also includes a hello.

Each of the patients we have chosen reacted differently to his or her fatal illness. Each one had individual struggles to overcome. Each one has had a different and limited support system, and yet all of them, without exception, had the courage to say yes to their illness without fear at the end, without guilt, and without unfinished business. It is fear and guilt that are the only enemies of man, and if we have the courage to face our own fears and guilts and unfinished business, we will emerge more self-respecting and self-loving and more courageous to face whatever windstorms come in our direction. As one of my teachers so beautifully put it, "Should you shield the canyons from the windstorms, you would never see the beauty of their carvings."

It has been our life's work to help our patients view a terminal illness not as a destructive, negative force, but as one of the windstorms in life that will enhance their own inner growth and will help them to emerge as beautiful as the canyons which have been battered for centuries. We hope that this joint venture with pictures of our patients will speak for itself, and that there are not too many words needed to describe what happens to them.

Our patients have been chosen at random. They were the first patients who volunteered to participate in this book, as a gift both to their families and to those unknown thousands who will look through these pictures and words and will contemplate their own finiteness and wonder if they, too, could face a terminal illness with such courage, peace, and equanimity.

Our role in their struggle was simply as a catalyst, to share a moment, a tear perhaps, a hope, and most of all, to lend a listening ear. Each one in his or her own private, intimate way had choreographed his or her own death; all were convinced about their own ultimate destiny and had made their own arrangements in keeping with the style of their personality, in style with their character. Each one chose to live to the very end in the way he or she found to be most meaningful—even our little girl Jamie, whose wish was to be at home with her mother, with her toys, with her brother, and with her prized dog. She, too, knew that death was forthcoming, and as long as she was able to open her eyes and see her beloved mother she was at peace. Although she had been in a caring hospital for her last treatment, she already understood that for her, at the very end, there was no place like home. She, too, as young as she was, drew a picture and reflected upon her impending death in beautiful, symbolic language which, later on, was a source of peace for her mother, who understood the message of this little girl and who was able to let go of her, just as the little girl was able to let go and symbolize her own death as a happy little balloon floating up into the sky.

I hope that this joint venture will lead us to think about life, about the way you and I spend our days and our nights. It will help you, I hope, to evaluate your own style of living and dying from moment to moment. It will show you that every good-bye is a hello, and perhaps it will help you, if nothing else, to share the deepest thoughts and dreams of others who have preceded you in death and somehow have shown you the way it can be for you if you choose to have it that way.

Human beings have one great asset over all other living things, and that is that they have free choice. We are not powerless specks of dust drifting around in the wind, blown by random destiny. We are, each one of us, like beautiful snowflakes that God has created. There are no two snowflakes alike in the whole universe, as there are no two people alike in the whole universe—not even identical twins. Each one of us is born for a specific reason and purpose, and each one of us will die when he or she has accomplished whatever was to be accomplished. The in-between depends on our own willingness to make the best of every day, of every moment, of every opportunity. The choice is always ours. When we have cancer, we can naturally put our head in the sand and temporarily forget it. We can drown ourselves in self-pity or in anger and anguish until it is too late. Or we can get the best possible help available to us in this country or abroad. We can keep it a secret or we can share the struggle with loved ones, thereby not only giving us an opportunity to grow, but giving the ones with whom we share it the opportunity to grow through the shared turmoil. To love is to give of oneself, and all giving is meaningful only if it is a mutual benefit.

In the course of a terminal illness, we can give up, we can demand attention, we can scream, we can become total invalids long before it is necessary. We can displace our anger and sense of unfairness onto others and make their life miserable. Or we have the choice to complete our work, to function in whatever way we are capable and thereby touch many lives by our valiant struggle and our own sense of purpose in our own existence.

From the thousands of dying children and grownups I have followed over the past decades, it has been only the ones who are willing to share who have left an imprint. The idea that we receive as much as we give has been the most accurate and literally true lesson I have learned over the years. Those who have not been able to externalize their fears and frustrations, their guilts, and their unfinished business, remain stuck in them. Those who have had the courage to scream and rage, if necessary, to question God, to share their pain and agony, are the ones who have touched our very being. Those were also the ones whose faces were peaceful and radiant when they left, leaving all those in awe who entered their room in the final days of their earthly existence. Those who have seen our patient Louise in her struggle to choose her own way to live until death will never be the same. They have all been touched by her example and will remember it when their own time comes close.

The patients you will see in this book became our friends with whom we shared much more than just time. If one is to be helpful to any other human being, no matter in what predicament, then the benefits are always mutual. Whatever we have been able to give them by our caring and sharing, they too have enriched our lives, and we are deeply grateful for those special moments and for the special friends who have made these pages possible.

Those patients and families who have allowed us to follow their final paths have chosen to do this as a gift to you who take the time to look at these pictures—not only with your eyes but with your heart and your soul. We thank our patients for allowing us to intrude on the privacy of their homes, to share their meals, their thoughts, and their hopes. And we thank them for their choice and their belief that they can touch your life as much as they have touched ours.

I · TO LIVE
UNTIL WE SAY
GOOD-BYE

The work which I have done over the last two decades started many years ago, preceding my academic career in the United States. It originated in Poland when I was privileged to do relief work in postwar Europe and came across the concentration camp of Maidanek, where hundreds and thousands of people were killed and where I saw the gas chambers and the trainloads of baby shoes of the murdered children. It was in this environment that I came across the little scribbles and drawings which children had done on the inside of the barrack walls. They often included messages to their mommies and daddies. There were also symbols of butterflies scratched into the wooden barrack walls, drawn with a piece of chalk or a rock, or sometimes scratched with a fingernail. It was in those days that I began to wonder about what we are doing to our fellowman and how it is possible that a single generation develops both a Hitler, a man bent on destroying the world, and a Mother Theresa, who gave totally of herself to help those dying in the streets of India. The question that emerged in my young mind was: What can an individual human being contribute in the raising of the next generation to prevent more Hitlers, to create a generation with more genuine love and less destructive force?

In those camps I saw dying in its most horrible form, but also living and surviving in its most gracious form. It was there that I met a young Jewish girl who had lost her entire family—her parents, grandparents, and siblings, all of whom stood in line and entered the gas chambers, only to be buried in a huge pile of human bodies. Miraculously, this girl was spared, and instead of becoming revengeful and bitter she was able to stay there and to help other people face their own fears, their own destructiveness so that they emerged as caring, serving human beings. What I wondered in those days was, naturally, where does this little girl get her courage from? How was she able to deal with her resentment, her bitterness, her anger, her sense of unfairness? And it was only after living and working with her and sharing with her our first aid stations, our soup kitchens, and our relief work that I began to realize that though there is in every human being a potential Hitler, there is also, in each one of us, a potential Mother Theresa.

My search in the years thereafter was a search for an answer to the question of how to achieve that potential, not only in ourselves, but in those whose lives we touch. People in the stream of life, in the midst of their busy careers, of their studies, of raising a family, of making money and worrying about the future, are not likely to search for answers to such philosophical questions. Therefore, the answers did not come from them, but came instead from the hopeless, chronic schizophrenics with whom I worked. They also came from the parents who had retarded and multiply-handicapped children. They came from mothers and fathers whose children had been brutally murdered, from parents who sat endless hours in hospitals or outside protective isolation wards where their children were hanging onto a thread of life and hoping to make it to another remission.

The answers also came from those people who were informed that they had a terminal illness and had a limited life span and who, then, often for the first time, took time out of their busy schedules to evaluate their own lives. They started asking questions about what they had done with their lives, and what they were going to be able to do with whatever time they had left. These people had the courage to look at themselves more objectively, through less-colored glasses, and they were able to put aside the unessential parts, the worries about trivialities. They began to get to the bottom of issues which we never face unless we are in the midst of a crisis and have the courage to look at things in painful but revealing ways.

This work of mine ultimately led to my teaching a course to medical students, social workers, hospital chaplains, and nurses who, as I observed, often had a desperate need to deny the existence of terminally ill patients on their ward. I would choose at random a terminally ill patient and, without rehearsing the dialogue, ask him or her to come and share with me what it was like. This was done in a screening or interviewing room, visible and audible to the students, who were not audible and visible to us. It was a private dialogue, in spite of the fact that our patients naturally knew about the presence of the students and were willing to share whatever they could about their own growth, their own wisdom, and their own understanding. It was from these patients that the now rather well-known seminar on "Death and Dying" emerged at the University of Chicago over a decade ago. I described the details of this work and its findings in my book *On Death and Dying.**

It became clear that in an institutional setup the staff still depended too much on the "death and dying lady," and that unless I removed myself, they would never have the courage to do this work themselves. It was far easier to refer a terminally ill patient to yet another specialist, the thanatologist. That was not the purpose of my work. The purpose of my seminars was to teach young students in the helping professions to take a good hard look at their own fears, their own unfinished business, their own repressed pains which they often unwillingly projected onto their patients.

Those physicians who were most afraid of the issue of death and dying never revealed the truth to their patients, rationalizing that the patients were not willing to talk about it. These professionals were not able to see the projection of their own fears, their hidden anxiety, yet the patients were able to pick up these feelings and, therefore, never shared their own knowledge with their physicians. This situation left many dying patients in a vacuum, unattended and lonely. One social worker made this beautifully clear when she wrote in Dr. George Wahl's book: "I know he wanted to talk to me, but I always turned it into something light, a little joke or some evasive reassurance which had to fail. The patient knew and I knew, but as he saw my desperate attempts to escape, he took pity on me and kept to himself what he wanted to share with another human being. And so he died and did not bother me."

My own hope was that more social workers, more clergy, more medical students, and more nurses would have the courage to evaluate their own attitudes toward these patients and toward terminal illness, toward the unresolved losses and pains in their own lives and that they would have the courage to externalize those fears and pains and anguish,

*On Death and Dying, New York: The Macmillan Co., 1968

freeing themselves from all their negativity and, therefore, opening up to the needs and communications of the dying patients, as well as their own needs.

After leaving the University of Chicago, I continued my teaching, first across the United States and Canada, and then later on in Europe, Australia, and other continents. It became obvious that there was a tremendous need which could be only partially gratified by my traveling a quarter of a million miles a year and talking to an average of 15,000 people a week about the plight of the dying patient. My house often became like Grand Central Station: Parents came whose children were missing, or had been murdered, or were dying, or had committed suicide. Terminally ill patients, who had been informed about the diagnosis and found their families unwilling to talk about it, found my phone number and address and shared their thoughts and fears with me by letters, over the telephone, or in visits to my house, and later on, when they became unable to travel, through my making house calls to their homes.

Many of these patients had been well taken care of in hospitals until they were beyond medical treatment. Then they were either transferred to a nursing home or sent home without the family's being fully prepared and without their having a physician available. It was at those moments when all the medical treatment had been exhausted that I became their physician. And I mean "physician" in the old sense of the word: a person who is there to relieve suffering, with a clear understanding that it does not mean medical cure, medical treatment, or necessarily a prolongation of life. The patients were more concerned about the *quality* of life than the *quantity* of life. We took our cues from those patients who were willing to stop all treatment and to return home, to put their own house in order—symbolically and literally speaking—and to spend the last few weeks, months, or sometimes only days with their next of kin. We soon realized that patients know not only that they are dying, but *when* they are dying, and they reveal this through the expression of a symbolic verbal or nonverbal language, like the drawings of children which reveal their knowledge of their own illness, their own impending death, and very often, the timing of their death.

We started to interpret for parents the drawings of dying children so they, too, could understand those communications and could respond to them in an appropriate way rather than with denial. We taught them how to make the final quarters of a dying child or a dying parent a true living room, and we used the center of the house rather than the bedroom for this final place. The reason we used the living room is that it had access to the kitchen, to the smells of the soup or the coffee that was cooking, to the window which might look out onto the garden, to the spring coming up, to the trees blooming, to the mailman approaching the house, or to the children returning home from school. We wanted these patients to be allowed to *live* until they died, rather than to be separated in an isolated bedroom. They had night tables with flowers that were picked by children, rather than monitors and transfusion equipment. There were no respirators in these living rooms, except for an occasional oxygen tank that would ease breathing and could be handled by a child who contributed to the care of a dying brother or sister and who felt that he or she, too, was able to ease some of the discomfort of the loved one.

Our research shows that 75 percent of the population still die in institutions and that the majority of these patients would be more grateful if they could be taken home to die. It requires so little to prepare the family and to teach patients how to be comfortable at home, without undue fear and anxiety.

In order to ease the physical pain of our cancer patients, we used an American version of the English Brompton mixture. This liquid analgesic that makes use of morphine, instead of heroin (which is illegal in the United States) enabled us to give pain medication orally rather than by injections, so that our patients could return home with a bottle of pain reliever to keep on their own night table and could monitor their own pain, telling *us* rather than the other way around how much medication they needed to be pain-free, alert, awake, and fully conscious until the final moments of their life. It was with the help of this Brompton mixture that we were able to encourage elderly women to take their dying husbands home and not be afraid that their shaky hands would be unable to give their emaciated, dying mate an injection. They no longer had to worry that the visiting nurse would not be around when their husbands were in too much agony and pain. With the help of G. Humma, a pharmacist at the Indianapolis Methodist Hospital, a handbook of the Brompton mixture was developed and became available to any physician who was willing to try this marvelous cocktail and who was encouraged to send patients home to die without the need for injections and frequent medical supervision. In all the years that we have used the Brompton mixture, our patients have been able to be comfortable, alert, and conscious, and we have never had an overdose or a drug addiction.

In the last few years I have spent my life as a physician exclusively in making house calls to dying patients. From consultations with relatives at my home, in motel rooms, in auditoriums, or in little rooms adjacent to the churches where I hold my lectures, I have learned of the courage of thousands of families willing to take the risk of removing dying patients from institutions, from hospitals, or from nursing homes in order to allow them to die where they can be most comfortable, namely in their own home, in their own familiar environment with their beloved family nearby. And by their dying in their own homes they not only help themselves but are able to teach a child, a mate, a sibling, that dying does not have to be a nightmare unless we make one out of it. Any child who has experienced the death of a brother or sister, mother or father, grandfather or grandmother, in his own home, surrounded with peace and love, will not be afraid of death or dying anymore, and it is these children who will be the teachers of our next generations, of our tomorrows!

This book will take you on some of our trips, on some of our visits to our dying patients, who are anywhere on this continent and abroad. For practical reasons, we have chosen only patients from this country. But my house calls have been duplicated in Australia, in Switzerland, in Germany, and in Canada: As we have learned over the years, all people are the same, and their gratitude is the same if they can only find one human being who takes an hour out of a busy schedule to sit with them and help them to die with dignity—that means to die in character and not be put into our own mold, gratifying our own needs under the pretext that we are serving them, when in fact we impose our own needs onto them.

All the patients, each in his or her own way, have expressed their own needs, their own wishes, and we have tried to gratify them. There are some who desperately need denial of their illness, but this is a small percentage of the population, only one percent. Our greatest service to them is to accept this need, to allow them their denial without making them feel guilty or unworthy or labeling them, consciously or unconsciously, with "a lack of courage." They have used denial all their life, and they want to use it in the final phase of their life as well. For them, to die with dignity means to keep that denial, never shed a tear in public, and we allow them, naturally, to live up to their own expectations and needs. This has to be their own choice.

Others will fight to the very end. They are the fighters and the rebels, often of the new generation. They are enraged that they have just started to live and their life is ended before they have experienced a first love, a marriage, maybe a child, before they have fulfilled their professional dreams, before they have truly lived. And it is important that we do not sedate these patients, that we allow them to ventilate and externalize their rage, their anger, and their need to try every possible medical and sometimes not "socially acceptable" treatment so that they are able to say, "I have had everything possible that is available on the market," whether this is Food and Drug Administration approved or not. It is not up to us to tell people what they are allowed to try when their own life is at stake.

There are others who bargain with God till the very end. And it has to be understood that the promises that they make to God are practically never kept. A young mother who prays that she can live long enough to see her children out of school will add a quick prayer that she can stay alive until her children get married, and on the day of the wedding she will add yet another prayer that she will live long enough to become a grandmother. For us this is the most normal human behavior. We would never challenge these promises, in spite of the fact that we know they will only be replaced by more promises later on. It is important that at all times we be in touch with our own feelings and our own projections, so that we can help and serve the patient and not our own needs.

Anyone who has witnessed a patient in peace and not in resignation will never forget it and will have no problem differentiating between an old man in despair who wants to die because the quality of his life is such that it is not worth living, and an old man who had found peace and acceptance because he has been able to look back at his life and say, "I have truly lived." So, let us go now to visit our patients in Cleveland, New York, and wherever our journey to them takes us, to see what they can tell us about their own lives, about their own struggles, and about their own peace which each one in his or her own way was able to find.

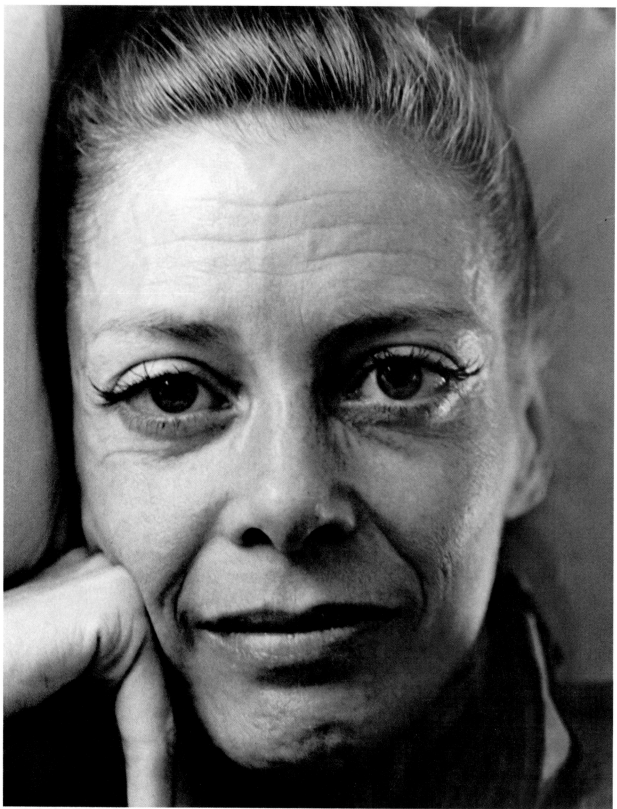

Beth, 42, dying of cancer

1/Beth

Beth, the first of our friends in this book, was a most remarkable and beautiful woman—both in terms of her outward appearance and her inner sensibilities. She was 42 years old when we met her and had been full of cancer for a couple of years. Pictures of a few years earlier revealed an outstandingly handsome woman, who had been a model in New York.

Her appearance was impeccable, and therefore, the cancer was a devastating intrusion, not only because of its ultimate fatal outcome, but because of the effect it had on the looks of a pretty young woman for whom appearance was of the utmost significance.

Childless, but surrounded by friends, she sought help from the best medical centers. She finally had surgery in Europe and returned to New York hoping for a little more time. Toni, her best friend and confidante, was her main support system. Lucy Kroll, her friend and neighbor, introduced Beth to us; the result was an all too brief but deeply moving relationship.

She managed to stay at home as long as possible, taking care of her own environment and medication without the help of a nurse. During the three months that we knew her, she had already stopped eating regular meals, was sustained by a food formula. She finally signed herself into the hospital just a couple weeks prior to her death.

Beth reading in the courtyard of her apartment building

Beth was also a poet and philosopher; she had spent many hours at the foot of the Soldiers and Sailors Monument on Riverside Drive near her apartment. It was a place surrounded by greenery, a place to think, reflect, and meditate, but also a place to be reminded of the transitions of life and the risks of life. It was a meeting place for young lovers and old people. It was not a coincidence that Beth chose this very place, which had been so meaningful in her life, as the place where she wanted her ashes spread after her cremation.

What Beth demonstrated to us is that when human beings have the courage to face their own finiteness and come to grips with that deepest agony, questioning, turmoil, and pain—they emerge as new people. They begin to converse with God, or the Source, or whatever you want to call it, and a new kind of existence begins for them. We have seen this in countless cases. These patients often become poets; they become creative beyond any expectations, far beyond what their educational backgrounds had prepared them for.

This process is exemplified in Beth by some of the thoughts that demonstrate the kind of person she became.

It is so nice to go out and walk in the sunshine, it just feels good to be alive and aware.

Beth in her bedroom

I have an appointment with my hairdresser and a cancer specialist. I know that my hairdresser will make me feel better. I am not so sure about the cancer specialist.

If my life is a gift, why can't I spend it as I please?

Death is staring too long into the burning sun and the relief of entering a cool, dark room.

She expressed belief that only real feelings can be shared and not words alone when she wrote:

Some people read what I write, they *think* they know me. Some people feel what I write, they *do*.

The reason for all this emerging creativity in patients like Beth is the fact that we all have many hidden gifts within our own being, and they are all too frequently drowned in the negative and materialistic struggles on which we spend so much of our precious energy. Once we are able to get rid of our fears, once we have the courage to change from negative rebellion to positive nonconformism, once we have the faith in our own abilities to rise above fear, shame, guilt and negativity—we emerge as much more creative and much freer souls.

When Beth's abdomen blew up and she looked like a pregnant woman, she did not brood about never having had a child. She picked a loose and colorful dress, put her hair up in a big knot over her head, added cosmetics to enhance her features. She looked pretty to the last day of her life. She always remained immaculate, contradicting the popular belief that all cancer patients have to look and smell bad. She was not too proud to admit that there were a few pleasures in life she was not able to give up—like smoking a cigarette. She never had to pretend to be other than she was. She never hid her true feelings about anything. She never had to be ashamed or guilty that she had played a game at the end of her life to conform to the needs of other people rather than to her own.

Beth, three months before dying

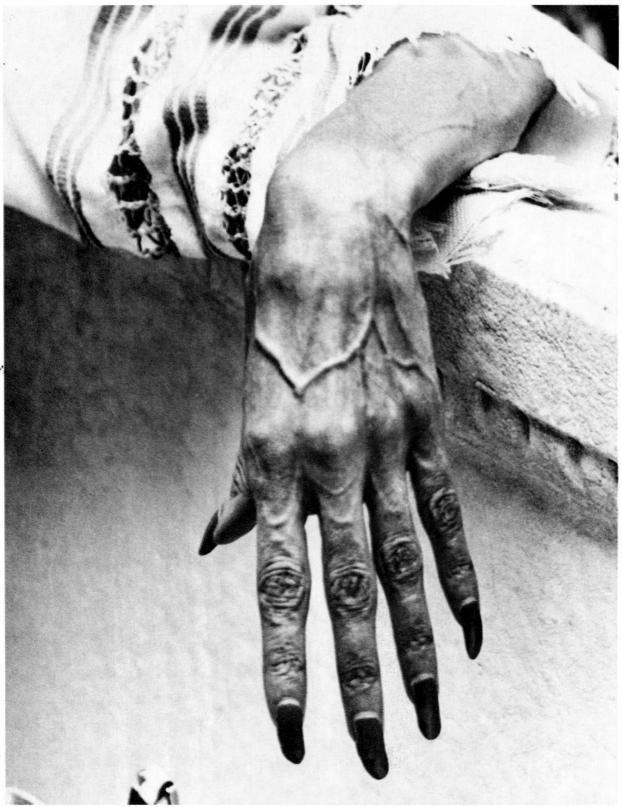

Beth, photographic detail

The kind of person Beth was is perhaps best illustrated in her own world of dreams and longing for a love that is rarely found.

You put your arms around me, held me tight and close to you and said, "If it be true you don't have long to live then every moment of every hour let's live them together. I love you and wanted to spend my growing old years with you but if you must leave me I shall remember you as something special I had for a little while."

That's the way it could have been.

When it was time for me to come home from the hospital you were so eager you were much too early. You waited with your arms full of lilacs, gave me your special smile and said, "I've come to take you home, my darling, now my life can begin anew."

That's the way it could have been.

We used to go out together every night but now I get tired so easily and would waken early to enjoy the long, beautiful summer mornings. You said, "Going out is empty to me without you by my side." So we would lie in bed side-by-side, holding hands, not saying much but sharing.

That's the way it could have been.

I remember those long early morning walks we took together. We were both filled with a new awareness. We gloried in the smell of grass newly mown. We laughed to think that we had never really listened to the birds singing. Nothing and no one was ugly to us because this was life, and whatever came later, we had realized that what we had together was special and it could never be taken from us.

That's the way it could have been.

As the cancer grew within me, my body became misshapen and ugly, but it didn't make any difference to you. You said, "I love what you are and that makes you always beautiful to me." Then I realized how foolish I was and fell asleep with a smile on my face because your love did not waver.

That's the way it could have been.

Now when we would walk together my legs would weaken but I knew I would never fall because you were there to hold me. When I would waken in the night screaming with pain you were always there and you would say, "Hold on a moment longer, my love, just a moment longer."

That's the way it could have been.

Sometimes I would say to you, "Why don't you go out by yourself or some of your friends?" And you would say, "Now that would be silly for me to do when I've got you to enjoy. I'm afraid life will seem very empty to me when you're gone so I want to fill myself with you now; that way you'll forever live on within me."

That's the way it could have been.

Once I was even foolish enough to suggest to you that you should find another woman. You got so angry, you nearly frightened me, but secretly I was pleased too when you said, "You are all I want or need, no other woman no matter how young or how beautiful could give me what just one tender kiss from your lips can give me."

That's the way it could have been.

Beth leaning against pillow in bed

Then came the momentous day, when we learned there
was real hope for me. It's funny that's the first time I
saw tears in your eyes, but your voice sang when you
said to me, "Deep inside I knew you wouldn't be taken
from me and it made me strong for you, now my
strength will know no bounds, we will fight this battle
together my precious one and we will win. Some day
we will look back on these nightmare days, your hair
will be gray and mine will probably all be gone, but
our love will burn as strongly as ever and we will know
those times of pain and sorrow were all worthwhile and
we still have each other."

That's the way it could have been.

Beth, on her way to the doctor

It is not important to know what the reality of Beth's life was in terms of the love she had. Most people are unable to understand the true essence of love. Love is not conditional; it has no strings attached to it, no expectations. This is the love that Beth, and those like her, was dreaming of.

Too few patients experience this kind of love in their lifetime and this is the hardest and yet most important lesson all of us have to learn. Those like Beth help us to get a glimpse of what it could be if we really understood the gift of LOVE.

Beth believed, no, she *knew* about the existence of life after death. She talked about her out-of-body experiences and said that death would be the one trip from which she would not return. She talked to her father while close to death herself.

She also wrote a little personal note to her father shortly before she died:

> Hi, Pop, you have been dead
> for some time now.
>
> Supposedly
> I guess I know better—huh?
> How much longer will you
> make me wait?

The last page in her book of poems ends with:

> What can I do with the rest of my life?
> LIVE ALL OF IT!!

Yes, Beth, you lived all of it and you have been an example to many of us. We thank you for being, we have been blessed by your existence, and we will remember your last handwritten words which say good-bye to us:

> Voices whispering, Beth, Beth
> You can no longer stay
> Hands reaching out to grasp
> Helping me on my way.
>
> I'll no longer ache with sorrow
> No longer feel this pain
> So adieu and fare thee well now
> I shan't see thee again.

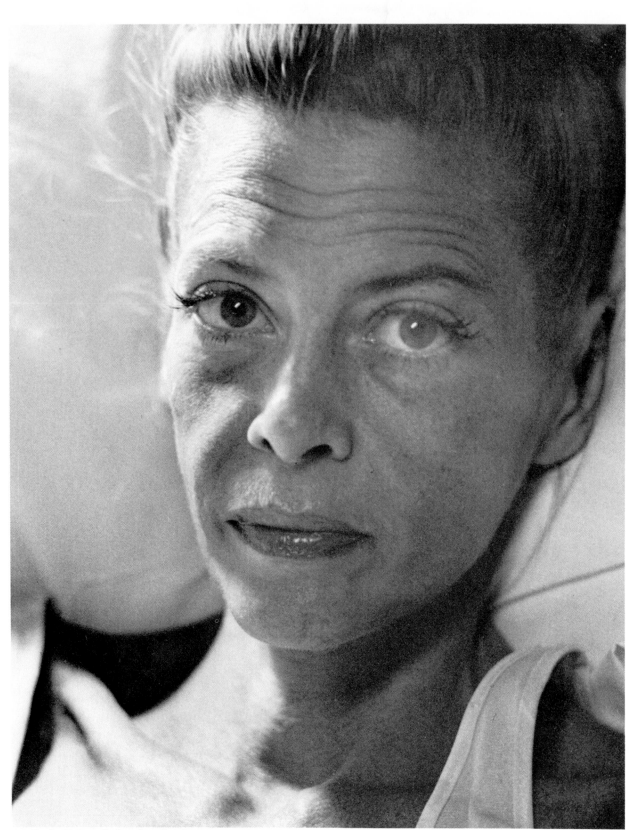

Beth, 5 days before her death

[*Editor's Note: These poems are from the diaries which Beth kept during the last months of her illness.*]

I used to have
Strange visitors
In the night
They no longer
Come to me.
I miss them.

LOVE
IS
Honeycolored laughter
Ambercolored laughter
Scarlet swings against a backdrop
Of freshly fallen snow.

It does
Strange
Things
Like
Dying.

If I could remember
    What I forgot
And forget what
    I remember
(with exceptions—of course)
I think
    It would be better for me
But, I'm not sure
What to remember...
                    Or forget...

Humiliation lies in the hands
   Of a beloved,
      Of a
          False friend
Better to have the
  Pride
Of aloneness,
A defiant end.

I used to wish for death
A lot of the time.
Then I died
For a little time.
Now I wish to die
Some of the time.
But, now I know
It will be
For all the time.

There is a sadness growing
  Within me
I do not want it so, but
  I know
I cry with bitterness
  Filling me.
It does not hurt the way
  It did
      Yesterday
There is only room for
  Just so much sorrow.
What will I put in
  Its place

      Tomorrow?

Beth's best friend, Toni, holding Beth's ashes following cremation

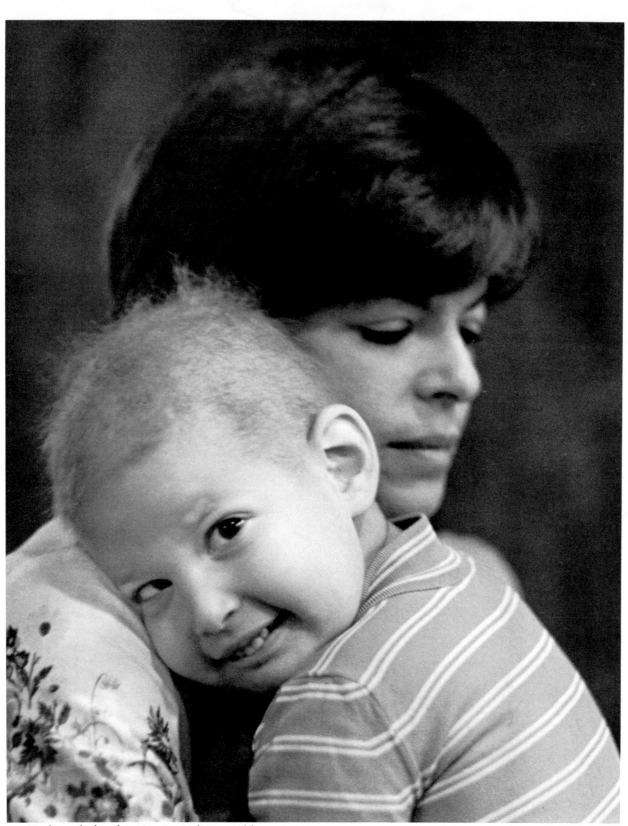

Linda with daughter Jamie, 5, diagnosed brain tumor

2/Jamie

Jamie lived in a suburb outside New York City, the only daughter of her parents and the sister of a brother two-and-a-half years her senior. Her parents, who were in the process of a divorce, separated just before Jamie was 5 and before the onset of suspicious symptoms. The diagnosis was a brain tumor, one of the kind that offers practically no chance for recovery. Her mother, Linda, who was alone with her two children, was aware of this but refused to believe that she now had to face the horrible predicament of losing her one and only baby daughter. It was hard for her to cope with the fact that she had to take her 5-year-old girl, the "sunshine of her life," to New York City for chemotherapy and radiation treatment.

Rusty, Jamie's brother, had his own problems, coming home from school to a house without a dad and now to a sick little sister and a sad and almost devastated mother. Jamie had lost her beautiful long hair, and every time Rusty wanted to play with her, he was reminded that she was sick and had to be treated with gentleness and care. He began to react to all these limit-settings and all these losses. And so it was difficult for him to cope with the many tragedies that suddenly invaded his loving, caring home.

Jamie was little aware, apparently, of all the turmoil that she caused. She spent her last birthday having her usual party with her girl friends and neighbors, who spoiled her

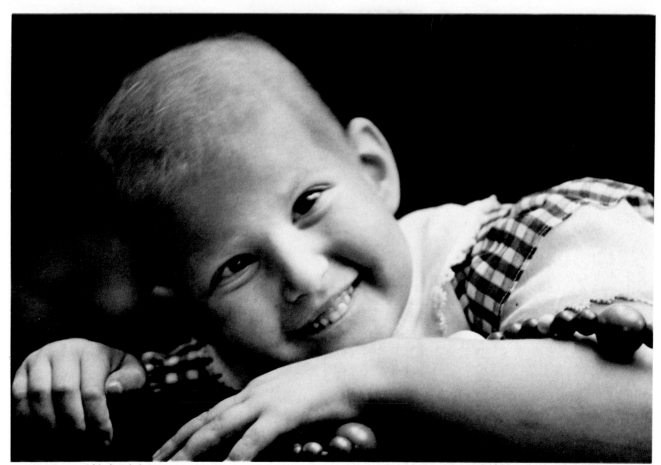

Jamie, fifth birthday

with packages and gifts. Mommy had made birthday hats
with the names of the children on them, and though Jamie
had not really learned to read and write yet, she was able to
recognize letters and she knew where each one of her friends
would sit. Linda put her on an elevated platform, she wore a
king's hat, and felt very important opening the gifts that all
the children brought. None of the children was aware that
this would be their last birthday party with Jamie and that
the gifts she received were of short-lasting pleasure.

    The only person in the room at the time who was fully
aware of the impending disaster was her mother, who tried to
make the best of this special day, who dressed her daughter in
her favorite checkered dress, and who looked at her as "Queen
for the day" knowing that this was likely to be the last time
that Jamie would be able to sit up and have enough
coordination to unwrap packages and enjoy her gifts.

Jamie opening presents at fifth birthday party

Jamie with brother Rusty, 7½

There were quiet moments in the weeks after the party when her brother was at school. Linda would pick up Jamie and hug her and look at her and, perhaps, for the first time, see the intricate designs of her ears, her bald tall forehead, her soft upward tilted nose, her tender lips which she pressed into Mommy's cheeks to give her a kiss. The depth of their relationship grew as Jamie became sicker, and as she needed more and more to hold onto her mother, to touch her and to be in her presence. It was hard for Linda not to be angry at a God who would permit such tragedies to befall a household. Linda could not imagine a time when she would be alone in this big house, surrounded by trees and flowers outside, and not hear Jamie's laughter and not see their favorite dog wiggling when Jamie came into the house to take off her wet shoes or to get a bite to eat.

Soon there were fewer and fewer normal days in the household and more and more days in the doctor's office. It was difficult for Linda to bring little Jamie to the hospital and see her subjected to tests, to being held tight in a chair, to being forced to follow the mirror with her eyes which did not coordinate anymore. It was difficult to see needles put into those tiny arms and to see tears and reaching out to her and hoping that Mommy would take her home and away from all these painful procedures.

In spite of the fact that Jamie was one of the fortunate children to be taken care of at Babies' Hospital in New York, where the staff was geared to sick children like this and where their open and caring attitude provided much support for Linda, it was painful to have to put her into the hospital bed with the side rails up and with the infusion going. No matter how many toys and teddy bears Linda put into that bed, Jamie wanted to be home, wanted to go to school and to play with the neighborhood children who had come to her birthday party. Very few hospitals were as caring and loving as Babies' Hospital in New York. Linda was allowed to stay with Jamie and even to share the same bed when Jamie needed that. Yet all those extra services did not take away the pain and the agony of a mother who struggled desperately to deny that her little child was soon to die.

At the time when Jamie had to reenter the hospital for more tests, the real despair hit Linda. It came when she was waiting in a cold hallway, with her child lying motionless on a mattress. There wasn't a soul around to cheer her up, no one to give her hope, no one to tell her that things would be all right. She was told, in fact, after a brain scan* that there was no hope for her little girl. She had heard of the scriptures: "Ask, and you will be given." Linda asked a million times for a miracle, but no one seemed to respond.

There were individual human beings who were remarkable, like Lee, a nurse who stood by her and who answered questions, who told her how to prepare for the eventual time when she was ready to take Jamie home. Lee showed her how the suction equipment and the oxygen tent worked. But Linda wanted no part of it. She was over-whelmed by the anguish and the agony, and unwilling to carry this burden totally alone. She was petrified to go to her big house, away from an emergency medical team who could rescue Jamie, give her air when she stopped breathing. Linda sat in hospital hallways, waiting and wishing to sleep, to forget, to turn the clock back. But nothing seemed to work. She saw her once happy, healthy, giggling, laughing, running child now lying on a cot, with a tired look in her eyes, with a bald head, with a tumor that was growing and growing.

With a sense of utter impotent rage, Linda wanted to scream, but there was no place in a hospital where she could scream. She wanted to hide, but there was no one who was able to take care of her two children. She needed to put her head on someone's shoulder and say "help me," but she couldn't think of anybody who could really help her. There were neighbors who would certainly come and cook a meal once in a while when she was too lethargic and too depressed to cook. And there were a few wonderful friends who would take Rusty out so that he, too, had a bit of fun and joy during a period in her life which she could never possibly associate with fun and joy. But, still, there was no help for her inner sense of loneliness.

*Jamie had a CAT (computed axial tomography) scan which uses a computer to show a "picture" of the brain.

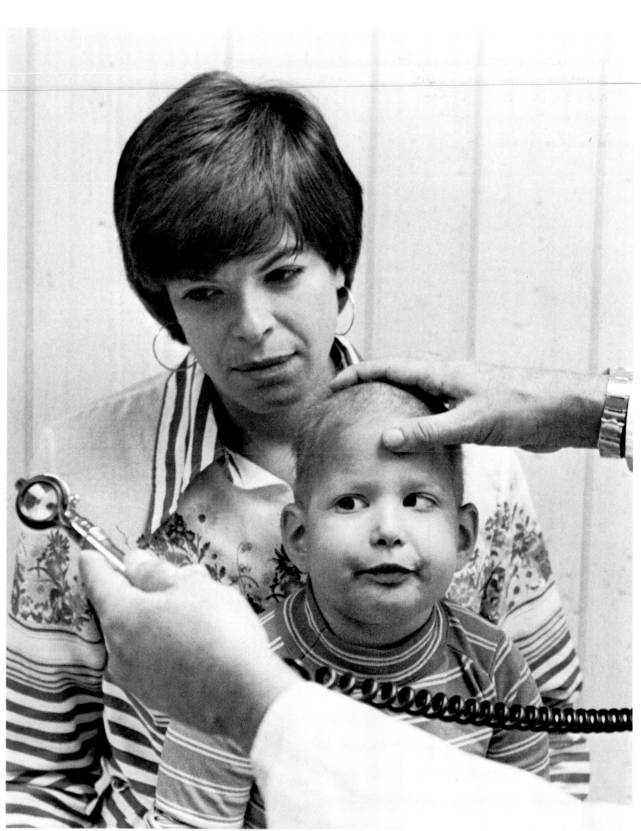

Jamie and Linda at medical examination

Finally, the day came when she took Jamie home. She made her a little bed on a chair in her bedroom. Their favorite dog was at her feet, and she spent as much time with Jamie as possible.

It was cold outside and, as it was cold in her environment, the whole house seemed to be cold. There was no life in it. She resented Rusty's difficulties. She had no patience with him, though she understood that he, too, needed someone to consider his needs. Everybody felt so depleted, so desperate, so alone. It was at that time she received a phone call from Mal Warshaw—who knew a friend of hers—and the promise of a visit from me. She had heard of my work, but at a time when the issue of death and dying was not relevant to her.

At the end of February 1977, the doorbell rang and both Mal and I dropped in like old familiar friends. Linda and Rusty were sitting together in Jamie's room, and though Jamie had become more passive in the preceding few days, it was easy to get her involved in the drawing of a picture and in the picking of her favorite colors. Linda, like most mothers during such visits, expected to withdraw to a private room to discuss the prognosis and the treatment. She had prepared the kind of dialogue that she would have with a psychiatrist and had little expectation of really solving any of the very realistic problems. She was stunned and surprised when she was asked not to talk, but to sit with her daughter and to draw a picture of her own. She used the same explanations that most adults use. "I cannot draw. I haven't drawn in a long time." But no excuse would do. She had to draw a picture, no matter what it revealed.

And while she drew a picture of her own desolate, sad, and lonely house, which revealed far more of the pain that she lived through, Jamie happily used all the conceivable colors, making figure after figure, connected and disconnected at times, except for the left upper quadrant where there was a free-floating purple balloon—a spiritual color—free-floating up into the sky, unattached and unencumbered. Little did Jamie

Linda, Babies' Hospital, New York City, at time of Jamie's brain scan

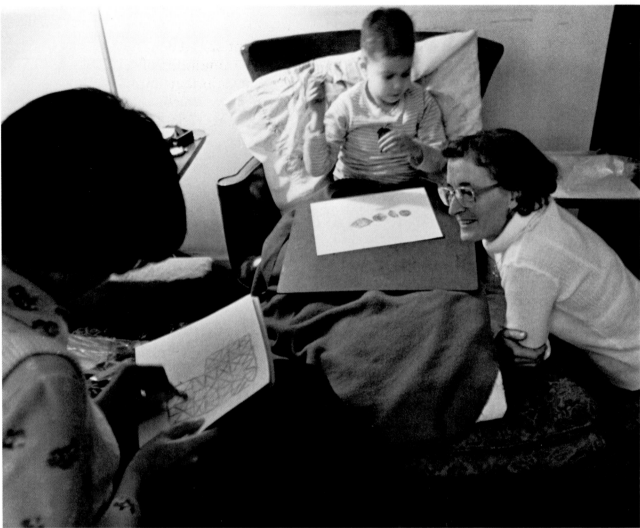

Linda and Jamie with Elisabeth Kübler-Ross during first visit. Jamie and Linda drawing

know how we used this technique developed by Susan Bach, a Jungian analyst from London, a famous but not enough recognized authority. It is a method that reveals the inner meaning of spontaneous drawings of dying children. In the spontaneous drawings, where there is a free choice of form, color, and design, these children very often reveal their knowledge of their own impending death and are able to share with those who understand the symbolic language the meaning of their illness, their life, and their future. The upper left quadrant reveals the far future and death.

In Jamie's drawing, the upper left quadrant showed that the concept of death was different from the remainder of the picture; it revealed an absence of fear and attachment and a high spiritual quality. Linda was intrigued by how much was revealed, not only in Jamie's but in her own drawing, and she verified much of the interpretation. It was this picture that ultimately helped her to let go. And in the following days when things were hectic, she would sit at her kitchen table, where we had shared a cup of coffee, and look at the picture which was fixed to the refrigerator. She realized her own fear now and her own inability to let go of Jamie, and that Jamie internally was already at peace and knew of her impending transition.

I was able to tell Linda about Jamie's thoughts as revealed in her spontaneous drawings. I was also able to analyze her own picture, her own loneliness in a house that had no people in it, no chimney, no smoke, no pathway, more like a prison than a home. Linda was relieved to share this pain without needing too many words. With a loving smile, Linda was able to say good-bye to us. It was a short visit, only an hour and a half, and though it took the whole day to go from my home in Flossmoor to New York and travel to her home and back, it was an hour and a half that was extremely worthwhile, knowing that this was all Linda needed in order to mobilize her own inner resources, her own inner strength to make it through the months to come.

There are several reasons it was possible to help Linda so much in such a short time. For one thing, when you have worked in this field a long time you become more and more intuitive about the needs of patients and their families. We are able to pick up the cues they give us instantly, both the direct cues and the cues that are often in a nonverbal, symbolic language. We also, of course, have the resource of their drawings and, when available, the drawings of the patients' parents or of their children, and of siblings. Another thing, and perhaps most important, is that we who visit these patients have no fears and do not need any formalities. We go straight to the issue, and if we are not sure about something,

Elisabeth Kübler-Ross interpreting Jamie's drawing for Linda

we simply ask the patient to tell us. There is a complete absence of superficial dialogue or of the kind of dialogue that often takes place during medical rounds in a hospital. Since we are no longer concerned with active medical treatment, we have literally nothing to ask except where the patient is at, what it is that he feels he is not at peace with—which leads us to the issue of "unfinished business."

When a patient has no unfinished business there is a sense of peace and of harmony, a sense of having done what needed to be done. It is like a housewife who has put her children to bed at night. The dishes are washed and the dining room table is cleaned, and she has a sense of having done everything that she wanted to do and had planned to do during the day. She can take her shower and go to bed. She has a sense of pride, a feeling of accomplishment, and it is okay now for her to go to sleep. That, in the simplest words I know, is the finishing of unfinished business.

During the visit with Linda I told her about my forthcoming three-week lecture trip to Australia, where I would reach other mothers and talk to them about the possibilities of care in a case like Jamie's. We discussed the possibility of Jamie's dying in Babies' Hospital, where she would get excellent medical care, and we also discussed the choice that Linda had to make about Jamie home to die. I told her about other mothers who had taken their children home and how well they had managed by making a bedroom out of the living room, where the children can be near a window, where they can watch the first spring flowers, the last snowflakes, where they can see the mailman or a brother or sister approaching the door. If Linda were to do this, Jamie could see Mommy in the kitchen cooking and cleaning; she could see the presence of a loving human being at almost any time of day or night. We explained to Linda that another reason for using the living room is that children often associate bedrooms with rather negative images because of the tendency grownups have of sending children to their bedroom if they do not behave with the statement, "You can come out when you shape up."

I also recommended that Linda rent a large bed that had room enough for her to lie in also, so that she could share the bed with her daughter and so that Jamie could sleep in her arms and occasionally open her eyes to see that Mommy was still there. I have found that this assures mothers of sick children of enough rest and also of physical closeness, and that it does away with having to climb in and out of a child's bed without any discomfort to the patient or to Mommy.

Linda and I talked about the possible medical complications that Jamie could face: the shortness of breath, the possible convulsions, and the need for a suction apparatus. We talked about encouraging Jamie to at least take some fluids by mouth so that there would be no need for infusions, transfusions, and other equipment which required needles and caused pain. We told Jamie to keep on writing letters and making pictures for Mommy. And Jamie

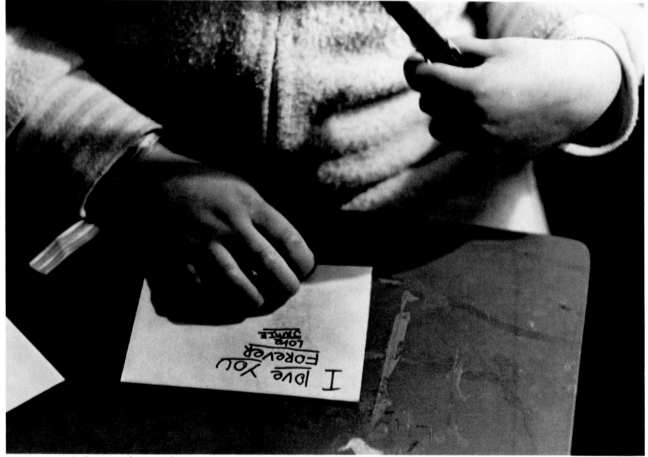

Jamie's letter to her mother

Linda with piece of rubber hose sent by Elisabeth Kübler-Ross

unknowingly gave Linda the two kinds of gifts that any mother would like to have. One was a letter to her, "I love you forever, Love Jamie." and the other one was the spontaneous drawing with the purple balloon in the upper quadrant which showed she was able to detach herself and float as a free spirit up into the sky.

Yes, Jamie had an awareness of death and of life after death, and was not afraid of it, and Linda gradually became aware of that fact and took consolation in the knowledge that if Jamie could have the courage to face her own transition with peace and equanimity, than she, too, would be able to mobilize enough strength to make it.

What still troubled Linda, as it does most mothers in such circumstances, was the remaining anger and anguish which she was not able to ventilate. In order for her to get rid of that, I sent her a foot-and-a-half-long piece of rubber hose and explained how she could find a safe and secure spot in her house where, when Jamie was asleep and her son was in school, she could express her rage, her sense of unfairness about the many losses that had befallen her, and where she could question God and express her rage without someone judging her or making her feel more guilty.

We use a rubber hose because, first of all, it is inexpensive, is easily available, and can be tucked in any bag, can be used in any place. It also enforces the power in our arms when we feel like striking or hitting someone in rage and anger. If no rubber hose is available, it is very easy to take a bath towel and fold it, or, if necessary, we can use our fists. But with a rubber hose the worst that can happen is that we will end up with a few blisters on our fingers. The main point, though, is that when a patient or a member of the patient's family feels an incredible sense of anger or unfairness, he simply uses the rubber hose and beats a mattress or a pillow or a couch, hitting that object instead of the person toward whom the anger is directed. He can then externalize and ventilate and scream out his rage without hurting anyone.

Like others who have used this technique, Linda was able to get in touch with her anger and pain so that she became more peaceful in the presence of her dying child. She even accepted the fact that Jamie had to be readmitted to the hospital for a final procedure, an experimental platinum infusion, which did not affect the tumor one way or another, but which the doctors hoped would slow down its growth and give Jamie more time. The infusion was in vain. Linda would sit for hours leaning over the side rail of Jamie's hospital bed, looking at her dozing and drowsy child, and she would struggle with her own need for peace and for unloading her burden onto an institution and its trained staff. At the same time she had a great desire to take Jamie home and simply hold her in her arms and allow her to die in peace, without needles, without equipment, without strangers, without shame and doubt, and without an alien environment.

This last stay in the hospital set off the greatest struggle

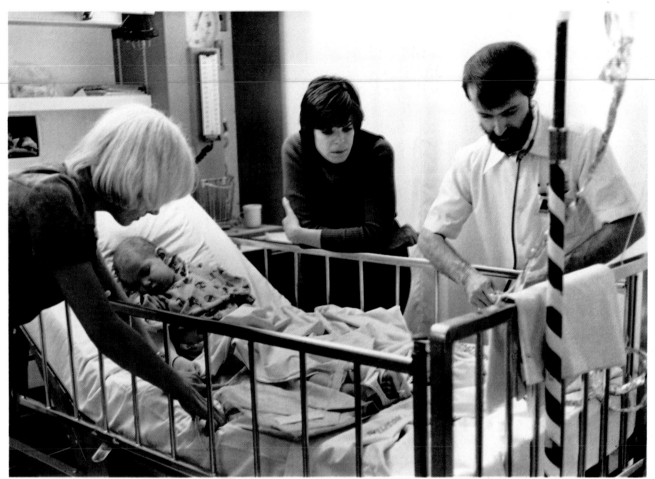

Jamie and Linda at Babies' Hospital for final platinum treatment

that Linda probably had in her entire life. There were times when Jamie opened her eyes and looked at her with a nonverbal plea, "Mommy, why do grownups have to make us children so sick so we can get well?" She didn't say that, she just looked at her and Linda would close her eyes, sigh, and struggle toward the final decision: Where was Jamie going to be? Where was she going to spend the last few days of her life?

There were times when Jamie would put her head on her arm and just lie there, and Linda would have given a fortune to know, to understand, what her little girl knew. And then Linda's mind drifted back to the picture with the purple balloon. And she knew that if Jamie had any concerns about

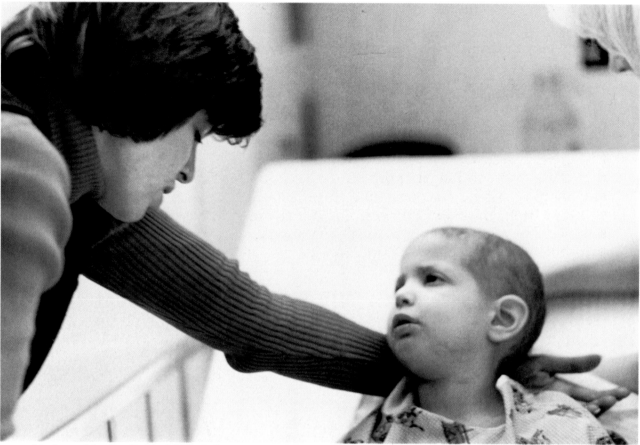
Linda and Jamie, Babies' Hospital

her dying, it must be a concern about her Mommy, about the pain she would cause the ones who loved her, not Jamie's own fear of separation and transition, but of the pain that all grownups showed verbally and nonverbally. It was the picutre of the purple balloon and our encouragement, our shared dream of her having Jamie at home in the living room under the big sunny window in a large bed, that finally gave Linda the courage to make the decision to take Jamie home.

Jamie was delighted. She would be allowed to go home with her favorite bunny, with her favorite toys. Her dog would be waiting for her, her brother would come home from school, and though she was sometimes tired of his noisy interruptions and his rather rough behavior, it would be good to have him there, not only to see him and to hear him, but also to know that Mommy would have another child at home who would make her laugh eventually and who would play with her and whom she would be able to see grow up. And all this was a consolation to little Jamie.

It was a consolation to Rusty, too. Jamie didn't shout and laugh and play much anymore. But she was at home, and that meant that Mommy no longer had to be in New York and that Rusty was no longer taken care of by relatives, neighbors, and friends, and he no longer had to be isolated, like most siblings, from his sister's illness. When he came home from school he saw Linda's face through the big glass window before he opened the house door. He saw her lying there on

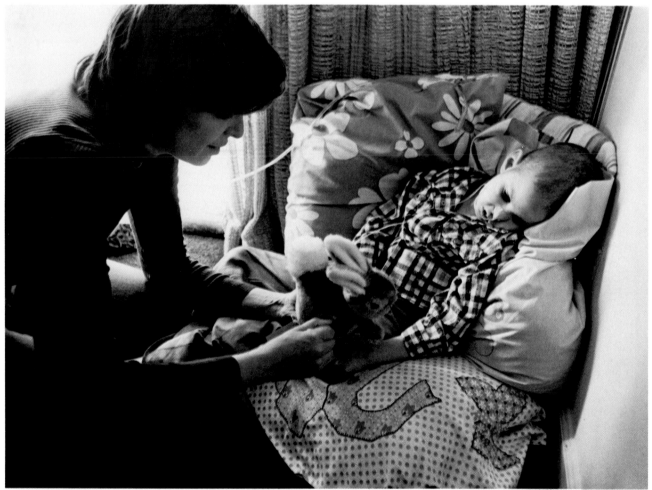

Linda and Jamie, at home, with Jamie's favorite toy bunny

Linda and Jamie at home with suction equipment

Linda, Jamie, and Rusty at home, 6 weeks before Jamie's death

the big bed with his little sister on her chest. And more often than not she had a smile on her face rather than a frown.

It was at the end of March, as we were ready to make another house call, that Linda telephoned and proudly announced, "We did it!" "We did it" referred, naturally, to her own courage and her own pride that she had decided to take Jamie home. She was able to get the big bed under the window, and together they looked out at the last snowfall, at the first greening of the trees, at the first sunshine opening up the first spring flower outside. Linda's face no longer reflected pain, agony, and anguish, but peace, pride, and contentment. Jamie knew that, and was able slowly to drift away into an altered state of consciousness, from which she opened her eyes only occasionally to see that Mommy was still around.

Linda and Jamie with Elisabeth Kübler-Ross during second visit

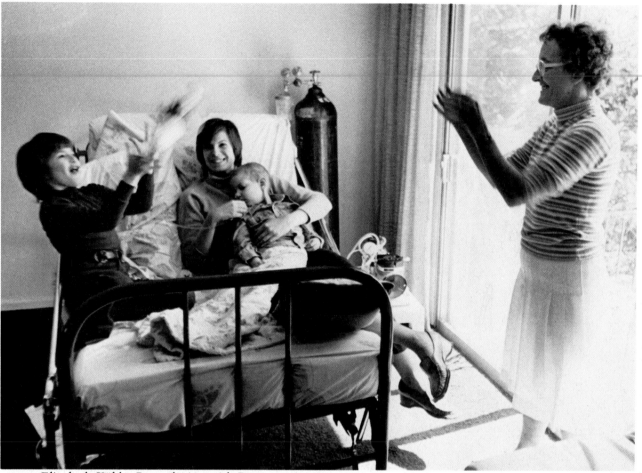

Elisabeth Kübler-Ross playing with Rusty

The most moving moment of my second visit was when Rusty came home, no longer a difficult, troubled boy, but a proud child who jumped up on Mommy's bed and challenged me to a game of ball with Jamie's stuffed toy bunny. There were laughter and joy and no undue fear that he could hurt his sister with the flying bunny that we tossed back and forth over the heads of Mommy and Jamie. After a few moments of playing, when Rusty had had his share of attention, care, and fun, he hopped out of the big bed and said proudly, "I have to go to work now." He moved to the side of Jamie's bed, took the suction tube in his hand, and proudly suctioned his sister. He wanted to show not only that he was capable of handling the equipment, but that he too had an important role in the care of Jamie.

Rusty helping with Jamie's suction procedure

After he suctioned his little sister's nose and mouth, he took the oxygen tube and gave her a little of the oxygen—again, simply to show that he was man enough to take care of his sister, so Mommy could rest and hold his sister while he handled the technical procedures. When Rusty finished, he went back to the kitchen, took a little snack, and then returned to his homework, content that he had contributed in part to the final care of his sister.

During our last visit, all of us knew that it was the courage and love of this mother that made it possible for her little girl to die with peace and equanimity, without fear, agony, and pain. In the same way that Jamie was born a few years earlier and was held in the arms of her loving mother, so now she would make the transition to yet another form of existence. There she would wait for her mother until the latter was ready for her own transition.

Jamie died on April 12, 1978, at home, and Linda treasures the memories of those last few weeks. We will never forget the courage and the care that this young mother showed after two single house calls, a total of three hours given to someone who not only needed, but deserved our friendship.

Since Jamie's death, Linda has reported to me that Rusty is doing well and is happily playing with the other neighborhood children now. At first he clung to Linda a little bit and preferred to be at home with her, but now she is able

Linda, Jamie, and Rusty at home, 4 days before Jamie's death

The last photograph of Jamie

to leave him with baby-sitters and at the homes of friends when she has things to do. Before Jamie died, Rusty asked if he could give her some things which she could take with her. He chose a book, a ring, and a toy car. The night before the funeral of his sister he went to the chapel to see her. They had put the book on her lap, the ring on her finger, and the car in her other hand. This was very important to Rusty. One thing which bothered him was the coldness of her body, and he told Linda the next morning that he dreamed he put warm water on her and brought her back to life and that they were playing. Linda explained to him that she was not feeling the cold and was somewhere else where they would not be able to be with her at the present time, but that she was happy.

Rusty decided that he wanted to move into his sister's room and keep many of her things. Linda was able to go along with this, and at the same time she was able to put away some of the things that her little son would not use. Needless to say, this short period after Jamie's death has been difficult, but they have been able to cry together. Linda still occasionally cries over some pieces of clothing or some toys or a picture that Jamie had made. Because of the shared experience, there is grief, but no longer any necessity for grief work, which is all of the work that usually has to be done after the death of a loved one when there is still unfinished business to be taken care of. This is almost always the case in a sudden death when we are not able to say good-bye to someone, when we never had the courage to say "I love you," when we are left with a tremendous amount of resentment, regret, sorrow, and guilt. And unless this is dealt with, most mourners will never find peace, the peace that we are trying to bring about by getting them to share and externalize their pain so that they can be free of such guilt and of fear and shame.

The beauty in little Rusty that Linda notices is that though he cannot easily express his feelings in words, the negative things seem to be outweighed by the finishing of unfinished business, by the blossoming of his personality and the independence of his spirit, which he is now able to share with her.

[Editor's Note: The following letter was sent to Linda by Elisabeth Kübler-Ross.]

January 19, 1978

My Dear Linda:

This is just a very brief note to say hello to you and to thank you for your warm hospitality during our quickie visit the other day with Mal Warshaw. I so much enjoyed meeting you finally and having the pleasure of seeing not only Jamie draw a picture, but you. What made me push you to draw one is naturally the fact that you, like most housewives, like to only look at the clean, pleasant outside house and it is most painful to look inside and see all the hidden pain, anger and anguish which we carry in our own "house." The fastest way to get at this is to look at dream material or at a picture and see how much pain and blackness we carry within us which we are all capable of getting rid of.

I am sending you by separate mail, a little piece of rubber hose, it is not meant as a joke, but rather a serious tool to get rid of some of the anger and the pain, no matter at whom it is directed since it all came from way back, when we were children and we were not allowed to express our anger or our anguish. Get out that pool of repressed pain and feel free so that you have the energy for the next year and can use it in a most positive, beautiful, loving and caring way, without being burdened down with worries about your older child and about the anguish and loneliness which I am sure you must experience so many times. I will drop by and visit with you again. . . .

Love,

Elisabeth

[*Editor's Note: The following is taken from a letter written to Elisabeth Kübler-Ross and Mal Warshaw by Linda a few weeks after Jamie's death.*]

" . . .In many ways, my life really began just before I learned that my daughter had a brain tumor. Most of my life before that followed a typical pattern. I went to college, taught for five years, married, became the mother of two children, and acquired a house in the suburbs. About a year before Jamie's tumor was diagnosed, I began to feel that I needed something more, something for myself. I became more involved in the parent-participating cooperative nursery school my son attended, joined a women's consciousness-raising group, and went into therapy. The growth and changes that came from these experiences may have helped to prepare me for the time ahead with Jamie but they also contributed to the end of my marriage. I was in the middle of divorce proceedings when I learned about Jamie's tumor. All of my excitement and plans for the future vanished at that moment. I knew that my own life would have to wait.

"From the moment of her birth, for some reason Jamie and I shared a very special love. I knew that she would need me even more now, and I needed to be with her too. Learning about her illness began the most profound and emotionally intense time of my life. Everything that ever happened to me before belonged to another lifetime. All my energy was now centered on the fight for Jamie's life. There were moments when I resented the limitations Jamie's illness put on me, but if she was to die, I had to know I had done everything within my power for her.

"I was told how serious Jamie's illness was from the beginning, for I insisted on knowing the truth. Although chances were slim that she would survive, there was room for a little hope. However, at the beginning, I found it hard to hold onto that hope. We suddenly entered an unknown yet terrifying world. The staff at Babies' Hospital helped ease the transition somewhat, but it was difficult to watch Jamie go through the brain scans and the radiation treatments. Yet she accepted it all and gave me the strength I needed. I knew that, despite my despair, I had to make every moment precious for her.

"Although I was no longer married, I was not entirely alone. Throughout Jamie's illness, I had the constant love and help of my parents and friends. Although they could not completely know the depth and complexity of my feelings, they were with me, for they too needed to do whatever they could to help Jamie, my son Rusty, and myself. At times I found it difficult to relate to these people, as dear and wonderful as they were to me, precisely because this was happening to me, not to them. They could leave me and return to their more 'normal' lives while my world was shattered. Yet I know I could never have made it through Jamie's illness without them.

"I experienced many moments of intense anger and bitterness. Despite the depth of my love for Jamie, there were times when I was so angry at her for putting me through this, for making me face the possibility of losing someone so precious to me, for depriving me of the chance to continue to love her and guide her and share in her growing up loved and loving. At the same time, I was aware of all she had given me in so short a time.

"One of the things that made it so hard for me to face my life without Jamie was that I did not believe in any kind of life after death. I had always been terrified at the thought of my own death, believing it would mean the end of all consciousness, although I tried not to think about it and certainly never talked about it. Many of my friends do believe that there is life after death, but I rejected their attempts to talk to me about this. I did not think it would be at all comforting to me if I believed that a part of Jamie would survive death. I was more concerned with the tremendous loss I would have to cope with if she died.

"Although part of me used a great deal of denial all through Jamie's illness, I also felt a need to try to prepare myself for her death. I began to read, beginning with Dr. Kübler-Ross's *On Death and Dying*. Perhaps my experience in a consciousness-raising group led to my desire to talk to other people who were going through a similar experience. Through Hospice of Rockland, I became part of a group of relatives of cancer patients. It was with these people that I could deal with the feelings and fears that I often pushed away.

"It's also through a member of this group that I met Mal Warshaw and became part of this book. I had been helped by so many people and I hoped that by sharing my experience, others would learn that they did not have to face alone the loss of their child.

"I met Dr. Kübler-Ross just after I learned that Jamie's tumor was growing again and there was little that could be done for her. I was in the middle of my own investigation of possible future treatments. I could not give up even though, intellectually, I knew Jamie was dying. Within a few minutes, Dr. Kübler-Ross knew exactly what I needed and, with Jamie's help, she gave it to me. She asked Jamie to draw a picture. It was Dr. Kübler-Ross's interpretation of this picture that was the first step for me in coming to acceptance of the inevitability of Jamie's death and a change in my thinking about death itself. Among the many shapes on Jamie's picture was a free-floating purple balloon. Dr. Kübler-Ross pointed out to me that this balloon's color, position on the page, and its lack of connection to any other shape indicated that Jamie knew what was happening to her and accepted without fear the transition she was about to make. I needed to know that the future would not be difficult for her.

"Dr. Kübler-Ross also knew that I was not allowing my feelings of anger and despair to surface as much as they should. A few days after her visit, she sent me a piece of rubber hose to beat against some sturdy object when I needed to get those feelings out. I have used it and it works.

"We talked about a possible way of setting up my house if Jamie were ever bedridden. That time did come. I had taken Jamie to the hospital for one last treatment. It did not help and her condition steadily worsened. She needed constant and complete care but she wanted to go home. Although I was very frightened, I decided to go along with Jamie's expressed desire. Dr. Kübler-Ross visited us again during Jamie's last three weeks at home and was so supportive of what I was doing. I came to realize how much I needed that time at home with Jamie. It made it possible for me to fully accept the fact that Jamie had to die. It also gave me a chance to do all that was left to be done for her—to make her comfortable, to provide her with familiar things, and most important, to surround her with the love of her family and friends. I too was surrounded. I could never have brought Jamie home without the love and help of so many people, my parents, my friends, especially Liz, Joan, Carol, Lois, and Lee as well as many others at Babies' Hospital. All of us, including my son, shared in caring for Jamie. It was especially important for Rusty to be part of this time. He had been shut out so often when I was in the hospital with Jamie or taking her there for treatments. He has some beautiful memories from those last three weeks—reading to Jamie, polishing her nails, or just sitting with her on her bed and holding her hand.

"I knew I had done the right thing in bringing Jamie home, but a few days before she died, I wavered briefly in my determination to keep her at home until the end. There were medical complications I was not sure I could handle. I called Dr. Kübler-Ross, and with only a few words she gave me the reassurance I needed. At that point, Jamie was in no pain and rarely awake. Dr. Kübler-Ross strengthened my newly forming belief that Jamie's consciousness was focused elsewhere but she was still surrounded by love. I knew then that I would not take her back to the hospital. It helped me so much to know that I could turn to Dr. Kübler-Ross at any time with any problem and she would be there.

"As Jamie's condition worsened, I tried to concentrate on the purple balloon and all it represented. I found myself wanting and needing to believe that part of Jamie would still exist somewhere, somehow, after her body died. During the week, despite episodes of respiratory distress, Jamie became very peaceful, and I no longer feared what was happening. I could almost see the purple balloon gently pulling on its string until at last it separated and floated away. I miss Jamie so much, but out of the pain has come much growth and learning. I no longer fear death, for as I held Jamie in my arms as she died, I saw nothing to fear. I no longer believe that death is an end. Even as I drove off from the cemetery, I had no feeling of having left my child there. She was with me as she has been many times since her death. In the midst of all the anguish are so many beautiful memories. Jamie's courage, her joy, her love will always be with me. She was truly a very precious gift."

Louise, 57, dying of cancer

3/Louise

Louise's life started inconspicuously. She spent most of her middle years raising her children and living in a small town on the outskirts of Cleveland. The house in which she lived for the past two decades is located in one of those quiet streets lined with trees and with small trimmed lawns, minutes away from a noisy airport and a metropolitan area.

Yet upon entering Louise's house, one was immediately struck by a sense of strong individuality. Her home reflected the special gifts and talents that were the evidence of the inner beauty she had earned through years of struggle. She had raised her three children, divorced her husband, and in her mid-50's made the transition from volunteer church worker to professional social worker in a local hospital. She developed and became Director of the first Social Service Department the hospital ever had.

As her children grew up and moved away, she became the lone occupant of the house in which she had lived for half of her life. This house became her refuge and place for introspection. It was the place where her two faithful Labrador retrievers were with her. Her home and her two dogs were her last remaining attachments and her great concern when she had to face the ultimate reality of her death.

When her cancer was diagnosed in 1976, she kept it to herself for a while, reflecting on the options she had, fully

Louise at home in Middleburg Heights, Ohio

aware of the advantages and disadvantages of surgery, radiation, and chemotherapy. In her work at the hospital she had helped many patients to face this same dilemma, and she was well aware of the general reluctance to deal with these issues.

She had counseled many wives who had been deserted by their husbands, or who were no longer "touched" by them, out of fear of touching a woman with cancer. She knew of many young women who hid the loss of a breast because of feelings of guilt. They had virtually stopped living a full life because of the negative and fearful reactions they had had to face in their spouses and friends. Therefore, in many ways, Louise was already prepared by her experiences as a social worker for what was to come. She had already learned many lessons from terminally ill patients.

The issue for Louise became the quality of life, not the quantity. What we have learned from other courageous patients was also true of Louise. It did not matter too much to her how many years she had ahead of her. What counted more than anything else was her need to live a fruitful and fulfilled life, to maintain her independence and to contribute to the service of mankind in one way or another as long as humanly possible. She also feared pain and dependency. She preferred death to existence in some dehumanizing nursing home, totally dependent on someone to wash and feed her, unable to have anything to say about what was being done to her. She was petrified of being "doped" by too many drugs and no longer being her own self.

During the weeks after the diagnosis of breast cancer, all these concerns passed through her head. She knew full well that to refuse surgery or treatment automatically meant, in the opinion of most people, an early death with metastases and pain.

Louise had studied the statistical probabilities, and finally, one evening while she was painting, a strong message came through to her: "Hell, no, you cannot undergo chemotherapy." She decided to decline surgery or radiation and to live life at its fullest for whatever time she had at her disposal. She informed her doctor, who had referred her to a surgeon, that she would leave her fate in God's hands.

What Louise did not count on was the great hostility and abuse she would have to face once well-meaning friends and hospital staff co-workers realized that she had not taken her doctor's advice, but had chosen to determine her own way of living and dying. They could not understand that a professional, intelligent woman could even consider refusal of treatment. It was considered "suicide," "ridiculous," "self-destructive," and "plain selfish," by those who, fortunately, had never had to make the choice Louise, and others like her, had to make.

It was after this decision, and the isolation and rejection which ensued, that I met Louise at one of my public lectures. We had lunch together, and in the middle of it she disappeared quietly into a back room. I learned afterwards that she had started to hemorrhage and that a total stranger at our table had followed her and discreetly assisted her. This

Louise painting

stranger later became Louise's friend and was to receive from her one of the first pictures she painted—pictures which were to become the outlet for her feelings, dreams, and frustrations.

Louise signed up for one of my week-long live-in retreat workshops. It was a week that neither of us will ever forget. Fifty people of different professional backgrounds, as well as lay people and ten terminally ill patients—average age of 28—attended. Louise suddenly realized that this world is full of remarkable, caring people. She began to see that she was not alone, to understand for the first time that the members of the helping professions are not intentionally cold, but have received too little help in coping with their own negative

Louise at home

Louise talking to visitor

programming and conditioning. She slowly began to see that they, too, had many fears, old unresolved hurts, pains, and guilts and that any mention of cancer or dying only reinforced their need to deny, repress, or avoid the issue.

In a milieu of total acceptance and security, their fears melt away; she saw up-tight people open up and share and emerge like butterflies from cold, stiff cocoons. The mountains, the air full of the smell of wildflowers, the knowledge that her beloved son lived nearby and she would have some private time with him and her grandchild, enhanced for her the depth of meaning and happiness of those five days and nights we shared.

On the last evening at sunset, we started lighting our fire. Fifty people once strangers—now friends—sat together in a circle and sang our favorite workshop song, "Wherever you go, I will go." As the group sang, one after another of the participants stood up and slowly with a great amount of forethought threw a pine cone into the fire—symbolically placing into the flames the one aspect of themselves that they were willing to separate from permanently. It was the beginning of a peaceful revolution on negativity, started by people who felt accepted and understood. They were willing now to face the pain of introspection and willing to rid themselves in public of whatever would hinder or impede them from living fully, and in a positive, creative way, serving mankind and fulfilling their own destiny. Louise, along with the other participants, left with new enthusiasm for life, recharged, knowing she would never again be alone.

When she returned to work after the workshop, the atmosphere was cold and another blow came. She was confronted with the "fact" at the hospital where she did her social work that it was considered too depressing for patients to see her in a wheelchair. She was prematurely retired, despite the fact that she was still very much in touch with her work.

Yet she did not allow herself to sink into a depression. She accepted the things that she was unable to change. She would not give up that easily. Slowly patients began to visit

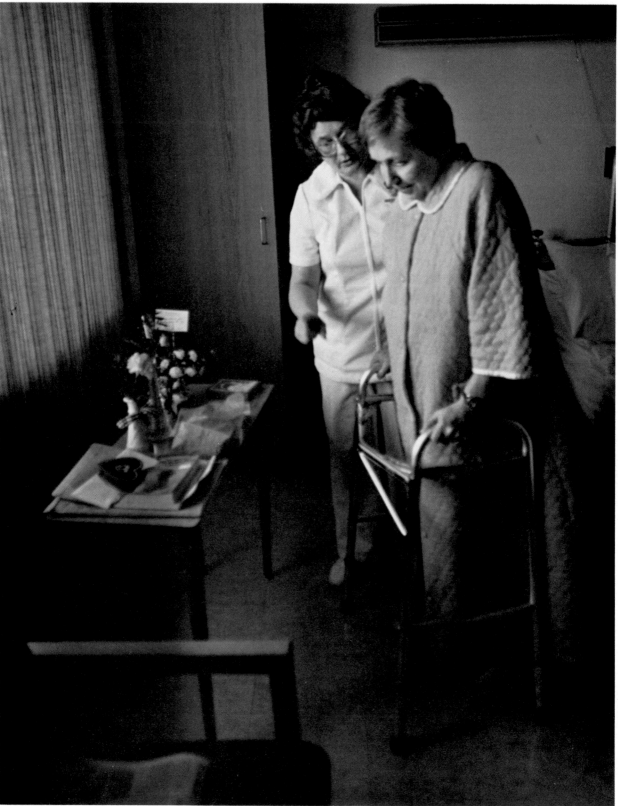

Louise in hospital for chordotomy

her in her hospital room, and later on in her home. Before long she had a truly remarkable counseling service in her living room. Terminally ill patients asked to be taken to Louise to get advice and sometimes simply to see her beaming, radiant, and truly shining face.

The following year, as Louise became more incapacitated, she began to live more fully. A card or a letter from a workshop friend, phone calls, and visits from neighbors and friends kept her in touch with the outside world. When the pain became unbearable, her physician decided to do a chordotomy, surgery which severs the pain pathways in the spinal chord and which resulted in a little relief. The operation was followed briefly by an unplanned stay in a nursing home, a time which she later blocked out and conveniently "forgot."

Elisabeth Kübler-Ross visiting Louise

During these crucial days Mal and I continued to visit her. We would send her little gifts which were symbolic, in some way, of our relationship—a little wooden carved Christmas tree angel from Switzerland which she hung on her hospital bed, or an Alpine flower pillow from my native country—a comfort to her when I was away and something to "hold onto."

Later on, when she "skipped" her drugs for a day and became more clear, she decided that was not the way she wanted to live. She discussed the matter with her children and friends and signed herself out of the nursing home. She turned her living room into a sickroom; her window was

Elisabeth Kübler-Ross with Louise's son Tom

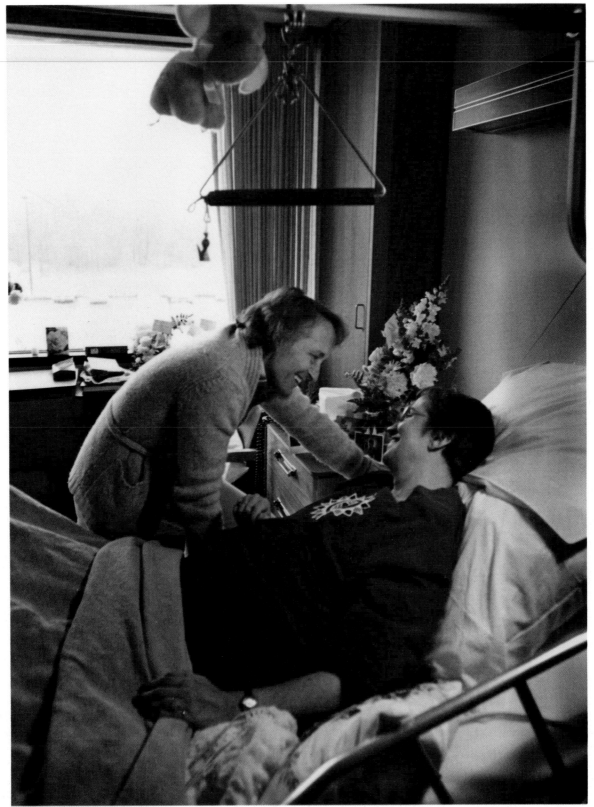

Elisabeth Kübler-Ross and Louise at hospital

Louise, Tom, Elisabeth Kübler-Ross, and nurse during hospital visit

Louise in hospital, with Swiss pillow, a gift from Elisabeth Kübler-Ross

covered with growing and blooming plants. A comfortable bed was moved into the place where there had previously been a chair, and she was able to look into the street. She was surrounded by her friends and her two dogs.

And so Louise, at this time of her life, found the courage to be herself. She did not despair when her children, unable to face her dying, became more and more remote. She did not drown herself in negative criticism when she was asked to leave her work and the hospital where she had helped so many. She did not despair when she was asked to give up the counseling at a time when her own life experiences made her the best advocate for her patients. She faced each tragedy with tears and temporary despair, but she faced it. She shared those difficulties with us and accepted our love and asked for opinions. But, always, she made up her own mind, she chose what she felt was her own way to cope with a given situation and she continued to serve in her typical loving way all those who entered her home.

During the next visit she was no longer able to be up,

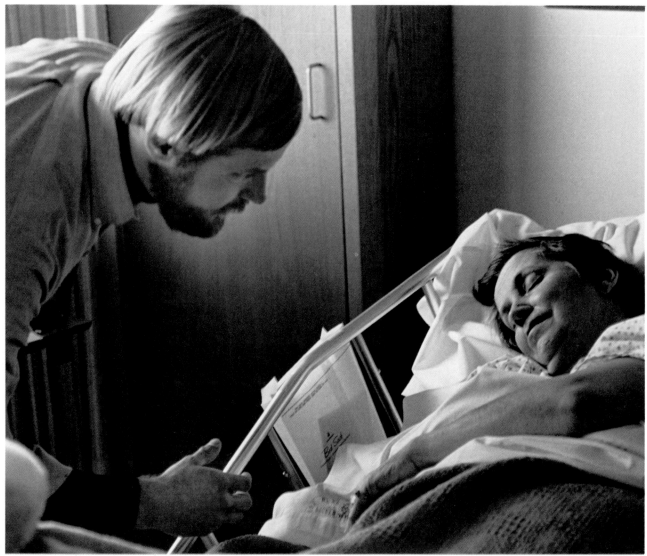

Louise's son Tom at bedside in hospital

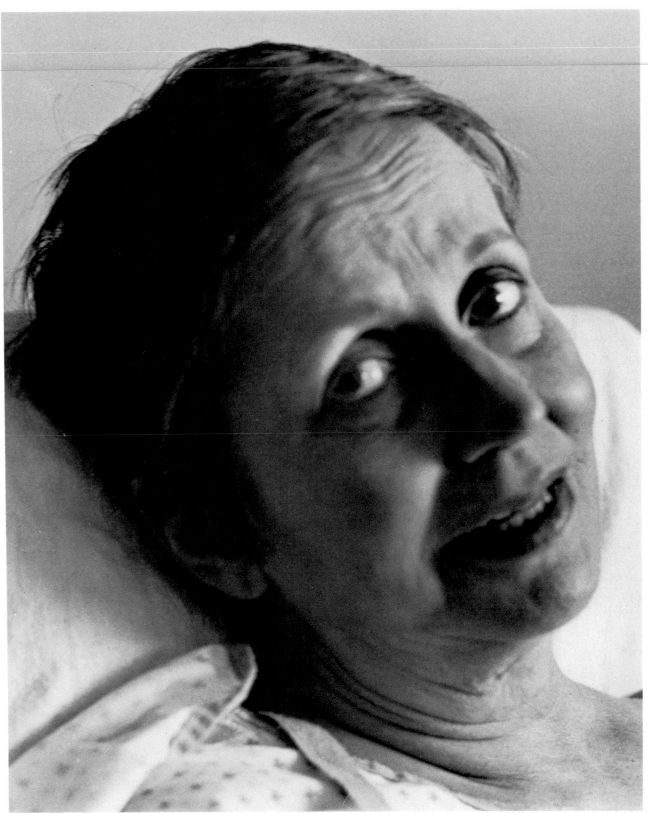

Louise, Middleburg Heights Hospital

but she continued to communicate verbally and enriched our lives by her own sharing. On what we all thought was our last visit she asked for an urn for her ashes and showed us the place of her burial. She asked if we would hold the memorial service for her and gave us her gift of trust and love.

She continued to paint until she was no longer able to sit up in bed. As with Beth's poetry, her ability to paint came through to her in the last years of her life. She painted anything from landscapes to the images of her guides whom she expected at the time of her transition to the next life. During the preceding summer one of her dreams had become reality: She had an exhibit of her paintings at Baldwin-Wallace College, her alma mater, in Berea, Ohio.

Yet a difficult and painful winter followed with endless snowstorms, blizzard warnings, and days when the street and everything else were snowed in, when nobody was able to come and visit. And there the snow piled up outside her window. Her two dogs stayed faithfully by her side and she would spend more mornings looking at them and remembering the promise she made to herself that the dogs would be put to sleep when she died. They would be buried at the same time so they would not have to adjust to another owner, and they would follow her in death.

Louise had more days when she drifted into semiconscious states and when her sleep became very prolonged. Many times her housekeepers would tell me that the end was near. They were not prepared for the reality that revealed itself in front of their eyes. After that long and difficult winter it seemed that Louise simply could not let go of her physical body. In phone conversations and during visits from me, she revealed that she still had some unfinished business, but she was not able to pinpoint it. Sessions we had at her bedside revealed that she had not resolved her unsatisfactory relationship with her mother, who was old and lived out of the state.

From my previous experiences with parents and their terminally ill children, I encouraged Louise to invite her mother to visit her, to discuss matters and to try to relate to

Elisabeth Kübler-Ross and Louise at end of visit

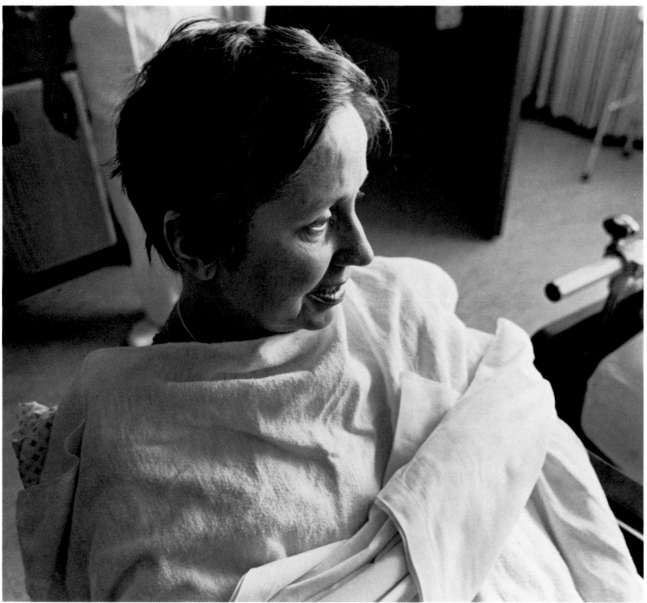

Louise in nursing home

her, no matter how willing or unwilling her mother was to talk about her daughter's impending death. The day arrived when Louise's mother came to visit. She sat at Louise's bedside looking off in another direction, not being able to find words to reveal her inner feelings. But they spent the day together and shared as much as they were ever able to share.

When her mother left, Louise had the feeling that she had revealed herself as much as possible under these strange circumstances.

A very few weeks later, she was not distraught to find out that her mother had died peacefully at home. Another chapter in Louise's life was closed.

"When Mother came to visit, I think she finally realized I was too ill to leave my bed and move to California. But true to her nature, she could not resist telling my girls, namely the women who care for me, that they spoil me and do too much for me.

"She avoided letting our eyes meet that night to encourage a real talk, kept her back to me most of the time and seemed to have allowed herself only a morning visit of about half an hour each day with me, when very little of importance was said. I had no problems with this. My business with her seemed finished, and I could be sociable and pleasant as I would be with any guest.

"When she died shortly after her visit, we learned that she had not even changed her will and had left the greatest part to her brother, which was only right, but one-third to a nephew who never saw or cared for her in any way. Others had done for her and had been near, but they were left out. She remained an enigma to us all to the very last."

Louise and I soon after discussed the possibility of her starting to write down some of her experiences, so that we could find out if she had any more unfinished business, any unexpressed fears or any aspects of her life she was not able to let go of. It is this letting go that is so important to so many patients before they can come to accept dying. Finances were her biggest concern. She was aware that she had enough for a few more weeks, that any life after that would have to be spent in a nursing home again dependent on assistance; this was an unbearable thought for this independent and always self-supporting woman. She was willing to take a loan on her house. She discussed the possibility of selling her pictures, and every possible aspect of support was discussed before she

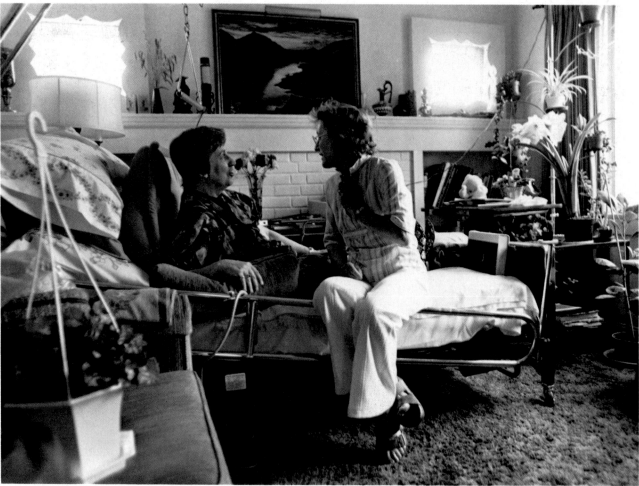

Elisabeth Kübler-Ross visits Louise at home

made a decision that she would be able to accept welfare support and a nursing home if that was the only choice she had left.

It was a difficult solution and a painful one after having spent half a century on her own two feet. But she accepted the fact and was able to grieve the impending loss of her independence. She put the final affairs in order, gave a few gifts here and there, a ring to a beloved person, a picture to someone whom she felt deserved it. She wrote little notes to other people who were in despair and thank you letters for those to whom she felt she had not adequately expressed her appreciation.

And she wrote to me, telling me about her most recent thoughts and experiences:

"Perhaps you may want to know about my concern of being too heavily drugged, so that I was not really aware of signing for surgery, or signing for the sale of my house. Surely in a hospital they know people are affected differently by heavy doses of drugs. One doctor insisted I knew when he came to visit me when I had been incoherent with others. He insisted I knew what I was doing and saying. If this is true, why don't I remember any part of it? Where is the fine line of being overdosed and recognizing that medication affects some more than others even though they're on the same dosage. I can get high on one shot of Novocain from the dentist. Wouldn't I be affected similarly on pain medication? How can you be responsible for handling your own business?

"About my own house. Once my head was clear enough to realize I was in a nursing home, I was able to start the wheels turning to get back to my own home. I fervently believe being at home rather than in a room with a senile patient on one side of me and an empty apartment parking lot on the other gave me new life. My two dogs welcomed me with a great display of emotion and very slurpy love and it was the best medicine for me. My helpers were dear friends and neighbors with an occasional nurse or an *au pair* hired to help me. It was warm. It was my home. I was encouraged to run my affairs as much as possible, but help was there if I needed it, to figure out my checkbook or think back over events. I had to learn to write again and also to figure some arithmetic. But slowly this came back to me and I am proud of schedules and working arrangements worked out with my help. For an active person like me it has given my life a purpose. I feel I'm teaching my helpers as we go along and they will be well qualified to help others some day. And also they will have a profession to turn to. The kind of help I have had gave my life purpose and a reason for living. So much different than treating me as an invalid expected to die any day.

"I wished, however, I would have shared my knowledge of the cancer earlier with friends. I feel the prayers would have helped me. The visits to a healer made me aware of Christ in my life and changed my counseling with patients and families before I left my work. This, I feel, was the

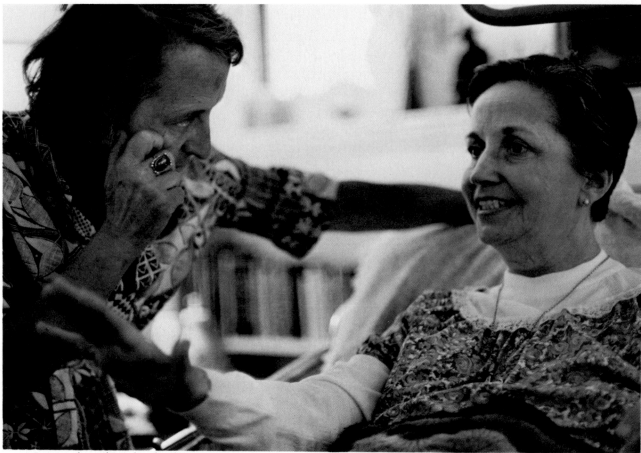
Louise describing her healing experience to Elisabeth Kübler-Ross

beginning of the small, very intimate prayer group that has become so very meaningful to me here at home.

"My phone calls from you Elisabeth, before you left the country to go to Australia, made me challenge myself about dying. I realized it no longer was foremost in my mind. And for a few days I was troubled over the events of my life. Friends who had seen me after the hospital felt I had certainly railed against God and my faith. I had ranted and raved plenty over my predicament. They did not feel I was taking my illness meekly. As I thought through what they told me, I realized I was now at peace with God. And although I did not want to remain bedridden, I was at peace for the first time.

"Sometimes later I felt, strangely, I could sit up in a wheelchair again, even stand. First, Elisabeth, my idea to

Louise and Elisabeth Kübler-Ross

Elisabeth Kübler-Ross presenting Louise with urn for Louise's ashes

bring the wheelchair from the basement was a big thing and it was perfectly clear in my head how I would use a board covered with contact paper to slide from bed to chair. It worked perfectly and I was again able to paint at a table.

"Next after prayer group, one day, I knew I could stand. This, too, came to pass. I stood very briefly with my walker. But I stood. Since then I've had a setback with inflammation of the muscles and misery with a distended stomach. But I know I will stand and sit in my chair again.

"Last Sunday morning, May 7, 1978, 3:00 A.M., I was awakened from sleep. I lay in my bed wondering what had happened to me, when a glorious overall feeling pervaded my whole being and I received a message, 'You will be well again.' I told my night girl but she was too sleepy to respond until she heard me telling the morning change of shift, and then she said, 'Oh yes, I remember you telling me that.'

"I told them again; I felt it was very important for them. I remember repeating several times so that they could bear witness to it later. I felt so well, so strong and healthy, as if I could literally leave my bed and walk. Caution, not fear, kept me from doing this. I did not want another setback. But the feeling was, it won't be long.

"And for the record, I would want it known that my breast is healed now, and I am aware now that my asthma hasn't bothered me for a long time.

"I wish the medical profession could understand what their visits mean. Perhaps there isn't actually anything that they can do for me since I refused the chemotherapy and other treatments. Yet I would gladly pay to have the professional person tell me I'm doing all right. It is very frightening to walk this way alone, and each change makes you wonder if the cancer has spread. Naturally, if I were taking regular treatments, I would be seeing someone on a regular basis. This way, one feels so isolated, they really don't want to admit that they know me. Can't this be possible even for a fee? I burst into uncontrollable sobs when my doctor finally visited. I was hurting so from simple gas pains. But believe me, a cancer patient never has a simple anything. They're always frightened by lack of knowledge.

"After coming to the conclusion I wasn't going to die as expected, I decided, 'Damn it, I'm going to start living.' New zip has been added to my painting and other activities. But now I've got to get some complete thoughts worked out as to how to make the finances stretch to cover my expenses. Once I no longer need the hired help, I should be able to earn enough to live. Maybe the way will be shown.

"About my belief in life after death. You asked for my thoughts on life after death. It's always been the same for me. And since knowing you, Elisabeth, they have simply been reinforced. I've always been comfortable with the thought I've been on the earth before. I had to return to complete unfinished work or carry out a message I had trained for. I felt at home with Cecelia and Gentry, my guides, and look forward to when we are together again for further training after my physical death. I do believe we continue to learn and grow both here and beyond until we are worthy of spending the rest of our time with him, 'The Source.' I am sure we will be with our loved ones for a while. As long as it is necessary, for that matter. But when we are ready to go on for further knowledge we are encouraged to do so for our next stint on earth.

"I am intrigued by the new friends I have since my divorce. My choice of friends is so different and the road we travel together so exciting, the relationship so honest and real. I feel greatly privileged. I firmly believe we have been placed on this earth to serve as the hands and feet of our Lord, to do his work which he can no longer do. He died for us to live and serve him and make the world a better place to live."

When the last snow of winter melted and the first flowers came out, Louise realized that the size of her swollen abdomen started to decrease and that the ugly looking breast began to heal. Her general well-being was an overwhelming surprise to her. She was slowly able to sit up in bed again, to resume her painting, and by April she was able to move outside of her bed and sit in a wheelchair. She was able to get her canvas near her bed and put her paintbrushes out, and she started to resume part-time activity which a few months before was inconceivable.

It was the beginning of May when Louise called me with a big happy-sounding voice, stating that she was convinced that a healing had taken place and that she was on her way to recovery. She was able to stand up for the first time in months. She had no more fears, no more guilt, and no more unfinished business left in her life; thus she was able to use all of her internal energy for the healing of her own physical body.

We did not know at that time whether this was the start of a cure of an untreated malignancy, untreated, that is, only in regards to the present knowledge of medical science. But it does not matter. For all of us who knew her and loved her, her strength served as an example, an illustration of how much courage patients can have when they are determined to control their illnesses and their existence on this earth.

Louise had received all the spiritual and emotional support that anyone was able to receive. We were able to help her, by learning from the help we had given others, to eliminate whatever negativity had been in her own personality, whatever unfinished business she brought with her into this life. And so she had freed herself of fear, guilt, shame, and remorse. It is known that there are four quadrants comprising the human being's personality—namely, the physical, spiritual, intellectual, and emotional aspects—and people can be well if these are in harmony. Maybe until the present time medicine has paid too much, if not exclusive, attention to the physical aspects of life and neglected the others. In Louise's case, we were able to complement that with the healing of the spiritual and emotional aspects of her personality. Together with her intelligence, her wisdom, and her own intuitive knowledge, she was able to bring herself into harmony and accept with dignity her last days.

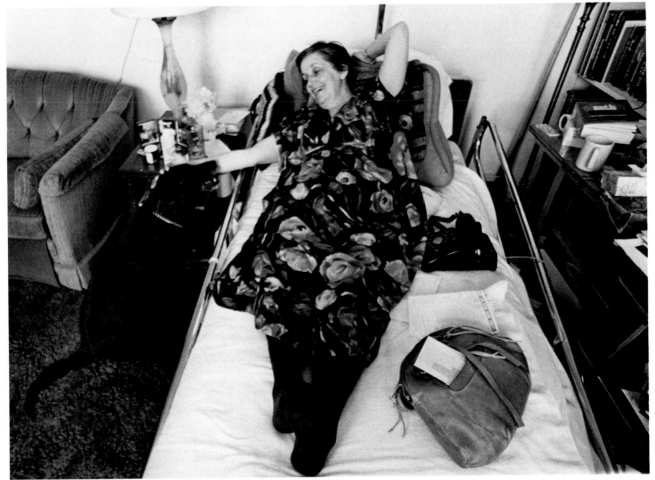

Louise, at home with one of her dogs

[Editor's Note: The following letter was written to Mal Warshaw at the end of May 1978, two months before Louise's death.]

"...This will be an attempt to fill in the spaces for you about my life. I was born in Cleveland of English-German parents, the youngest of three children, and got my first taste and love for nature and reading from my father. I was married at 21 and, as many did, followed my husband around the army camps in the States as long as I could until he was sent to South America during WWII. Our first baby was born in 1944 and her father didn't see her until she was one year old. I dutifully raised my children until I was able to sandwich classes in at night from a nearby college and that is when my world began to open up. An outstanding, understanding minister trained me to be a church-visitor, which in actuality was the first training for my social work in the hospital. Our vacations were spent camping—again outdoors enjoying nature. My husband was well-versed in the flora and fauna, greatly increasing the love I already had for nature. I owe him so much for what he taught me, so that when I knew I had cancer it was the only thing that sustained me, and I tried so hard to see and smell and feel all I could while I was still alive and, as it turned out, before I was confined to my bed. I want so to thank him for what he did teach me but it was never easy to thank him for anything—it would immediately be cut off—and now that we're divorced, it's even harder since, as they say, he belongs to someone else, and I wouldn't want the gesture misunderstood.

"I nibbled at classes at Baldwin-Wallace College in the evenings at first, until friends helped me financially and psychologically to finish the last two years. I graduated in 1972, getting my Bachelor of Arts in Sociology with a minor in Psychology. This education led me to my work as a social worker in the local hospital. I was given the honor of setting up the first Social Service Department and appointed Director of Social Services. I learned early that the physicians and families of patients were looking for local resources for their ongoing needs and it became the Department's specialty to gather the resources as we assisted with discharge planning.

The Department was a little precocious for some of the administration who had never worked with social workers, but those that had helped make the position wonderful, a combination of church and social work. The position was ideal—made to order for me, and you can well imagine my keen disappointment when I could no longer handle the work, and the weather made the bone cancer too painful to go out each day.

"My first reaction to hearing I had developed the second lump was typical. (The first lump was on the opposite breast and a lumpectomy was performed to remove it.) After the lumpectomy I was fine in the hospital—visiting patients in my bathrobe, doing my social work—and the nurses and doctor were very supportive, but I realized, after getting home, that without that supportive team I never would face a mastectomy. My husband would not look at the tiny scar where my lumpectomy was performed and I was totally alone with it. The following year I told him of the doctor's report that I had just received that I had the second lump and he simply couldn't look at me as I sat crying in the rocking chair. He watched the TV commercial and went back to his magazine to read and never ever held me or soothed me or consoled me. Then and there I decided on the divorce rather than live in anger and resentment toward this man. It wasn't until much later that I could understand this man's need to run away from this kind of news. I didn't consider his needs.

"I didn't go to the surgeon as recommended by my doctor and it wasn't until I came down with flu that winter that the doctor heard I didn't want to be admitted to the hospital—I didn't want my medical history to mention the cancer, which by now was a sizable lump larger than a half dollar. When the doctor did finally see the lump I asked him not to give me false hope, and as he sank down in his chair he just said, 'Mrs. D, I don't offer you any hope, and it will probably break through very soon.' Because he was so kind I agreed to try chemotherapy and had the prescription filled that day. I was expecting weekend company so planned to start the medication on Monday. Friday evening I decided to paint as I usually did, but instead of turning on the radio to dance and sing to as I painted, I put on my records of the 'Messiah' and as I painted I suddenly *felt* the overwhelming message, 'Hell, no, you can't take that medication!' I called a friend who was a psychologist to ask what he thought was happening to me. We agreed that it was my true gut reaction and that I should follow along with it.

"The following Monday, I explained to my doctor why I couldn't take the medication and he just sadly nodded his head. His own father had cancer and was asking to be permitted to go without medication and hopefully together we would help the doctor understand how patients feel.

"Working at the hospital one soon learned death is not reserved for the aged, nor is it fair in the type of illness it wishes on its victims. I don't believe I ever reached the 'why me' stage. I saw too many without a reason why. I have never been afraid to die, feeling I would be returning 'home', therefore death was a friendly but not totally understood place for me.

"Through some literature sent to department heads at the hospital, I learned of Elisabeth's Life-Death and Transition workshop in Sylvania, Ohio, and was the only one with cancer attending the workshop. I had already read her book *On Death and Dying*.

"As I look back at this first workshop I remember Elisabeth being very quietly supportive to me—not when everyone else rushed in to insist I have a mastectomy, but rather to ask how she could be supportive in whatever way I had chosen to handle the cancer. When my eyes met hers as she talked of life after death we both knew we had been there before and understood each other. After that we were like sisters.

"After the workshop with Elisabeth I read many of the books she had suggested on the booklist at the workshop. It reinforced my feelings and made me look forward to what was waiting for me, as I fervently believed there was ongoing life awaiting each of us.

"I later painted the drawing I did at the workshop and sold it to my attorney for $300.

"Elisabeth has turned into a wonderful friend who

shares many of my beliefs and permits me to share her wonderful enlightened version of what the near future brings. She has come at times when I was experiencing the worst pain, at inconvenience to herself, and has been great strength to me through the various stages of the illness.

"After the workshop and reading so many of the books on Elisabeth's reading list I naturally shared my excitement, wonder and thoughts with close friends and a whole new world of thought opened to me—much deeper than I had ever gone before in thinking about life after death. It was exciting to speculate upon what might be, and the thought of death took on a different dimension all wrapped up with reincarnation; and there was no longer the fear of the unknown but the certainty I had been here before and life does go on. Naturally this could not be communicated verbally with my patients but, since I was now attuned to hearing what was not heard before, I 'heard' patients who believed as I did and the look in their eyes when we said 'good-bye' convinced me they knew as well as I did that we would meet again.

"After a visit from Elisabeth one time (last year), she said she would like to give me a gift and invited me to an overnight visit with her friends who joined her in her life-after-death research. I stayed only overnight but what those few hours meant to me! It was there that I had a rare and unique opportunity to get in touch with my own guides and soulmates, Gentry and Cecelia. They permitted me to touch them and then escorted me into a private little room (without the aid of my walker) for a private talk to have any questions answered, about life before as well as hereafter, that they could. It was a warm, very loving relationship between the three of us and it was then I was told that Cecelia is the one who helps me with my painting. I had never painted before 1973 and if ever I drew anything it was stick-people only. Now after a Christmas gift of an oil painting set, I was turning out beautiful pictures of all kinds—no one specialty—and with only a few sessions with a local night art class. Nothing was impossible, from portraits to landscapes.

"My oldest son, Tom, had been the closest of the three

children during my illness. Due to his experience with death in Vietnam and his own close brush with death there, it was easier to talk to him about my illness and impending death. When I was hospitalized he was free to be with me the most, and I feel the load was put on him to make decisions for me that he later learned I remembered nothing about, even though we had discussed them at great length in the hospital—for instance, selling my home and going to the nursing home. It was a heavy load he didn't shirk, especially since we had not discussed any of my plans earlier. Later his brother Paul was able to leave work and relieve Tom at times when I was in the nursing home. It was a heartrending experience for them both. Paul had not ever been exposed to death of loved ones as Tom had, and my not recognizing him (because I was so drugged) tore him apart. We had all been especially close and it was a difficult experience for the children—especially leaving me in a nursing home. My daughter was involved in problems of her own that none of us knew about and left the responsibility of handling me to the boys. Tom remained with me until I returned to my home and had adequate help to be with me.

"During one of Elisabeth's many visits she asked if there was anything she could do for me, as she always did. I had been thinking of my funeral plans and the only part unfinished was the actual urn for my ashes. Elisabeth traveled to so many different and exotic places I thought she could surely find the kind of urn I was interested in; besides, what closer, dearer friend could I think of to have purchase my urn for me. It was like having her hold my hand all of the way. From the very beginning, through the various stages of growth, not only for my patients but for myself, she had been the one to turn to. I felt privileged that she would take her time to shop for me. How much I had changed, from stumbling and struggling to accept my condition, I had reached the point where friends could calmly talk about the only plans left to complete, buying the urn for my ashes. And I knew I was free to ask her to shop for me. That is friendship!

[Editor's Note: Louise died in July of 1978. At a memorial service on July 22, Elisabeth Kübler-Ross offered the following reflections:]

My last promise to Louise was to be here today and—I guess to share with you the meaning of her illness and her final months, which have been quite unusual and very special as Louise was very special and unique to all of us.

She has become a symbol and example of what it is like to make use of the human right *of free choice.*

She not only chose to serve her church and her hospital patients, she also made the not so easy decision to accept her diagnosis of cancer and *to live with it.* She literally lived with it; she loved her body and chose not to have surgery—her survival far exceeded all medical and scientific expectation. But it is not only the quantity of time Louise had, in spite of the fact that she chose not to accept any conventional treatment, it is what she made out of this extra time that made Louise an example to all of us and the many whose lives she has touched and the hundreds of thousands she will touch in the future.

Instead of becoming bitter when she was prematurely retired, she saw needy people and frightened patients in her home and made a blessing out of it.

Instead of going through a series of surgeries, chemotherapy or radiation, she used her own inner, positive energy, love, and her own healing power to control the speeding of the malignancy.

Instead of becoming despondent and depressed over her inability to get around, she fixed her home up in such a way that she was able to function to the very end and to become an inspiration to all who entered there.

Instead of allowing others to put her in a hospital or nursing home, sedated and dependent, she signed herself out and started to paint at home, living long enough to see her work exhibited and to share many of her paintings with those she loved.

As she blessed others by her existence, she was blessed by her children, her friends and neighbors who did not desert her, but especially by the very loving ladies who took over her final care at home, gave her not only physical care, but were more like guardian angels surrounding her with tender, loving care and seeing that her needs were met cheerfully and efficiently. I want to thank them for this example of unconditional love!

As Louise lived so she died—a strong believer, knowing her heavenly guidance personally and looking forward to her transition—she postponed her death long enough to be able to read the whole manuscript of our book about her. When I sat by her side she approved this text and the book jacket—her shining face on it—knowing that the book will be published at Christmas and that it will not only be a testament to her valiant struggle but also her gift to the world, an example of great acceptance, not only for others but also for herself—*ALL of herself*—intellect, emotion, spirit and physical aspects of herself including her cancer.

On her behalf I would like to say to all of you present she has been blessed by your existence as we have been blessed by hers.

II · ALTERNATIVES TO HOSPITAL CARE

Jack, 72, cancer patient

1/Jack

Jack is a 71-year-old-man with a history of cancer of the liver. He also has cellulitis and ulcerated feet and legs. He has trouble walking now. He has also had a long history of alcoholism and, in many ways, a hard and difficult life. Jack earned his living as a construction worker and apartment house superintendent. He lived through the death of his son, who died of lung cancer two days before my visit with him at St. Rose's Home, run by the Hawthorne Dominicans for the care of incurable cancer patients, in New York City. Jack was admitted there in July of 1976 after being in a New York hospital, where he was given two weeks to live.

He had arrived at the hospital in a deteriorated condition and with an extremely poor outlook on life, not only physically, but emotionally and spiritually. His second wife, Agnes, visited him regularly at the hospital and had very little hope of having much time left with her husband. Yet after admission to St. Rose's, he began to improve. He received regular meals there and the Sisters tried to encourage him to change his lifestyle, making him interested in living and supporting him in whatever ways they were able to. He received massive pain medication and loving care, and slowly and gradually he started to become interested in activities outside of his bed. He was impressed, as most people are, that St. Rose's served liquor and beer and that he was able to stop excessive alcohol intake and stick to regular healthful meals.

Jack in his workshop at St. Rose's Home in New York City

When I talked with Jack, I was impressed by this man who looked so well in every respect except for his inability to mobilize himself much. He was sitting in a wheelchair, seemed sociable and friendly, and seemed to have a sense of great pride. He showed me the dollhouse that he had started to make. These dollhouses not only kept him busy and occupied, but brought much happiness and joy to a great number of children. He used the occupational therapy room in St. Rose's, a room with big windows, plants on the windowsills, and a beautiful view out onto the river in New York City. The table was full of paints and other materials.

Jack working on one of his dollhouses

Photographic detail, Jack working on doll house

Jack in workshop finishing dollhouse

Anyone looking at Jack's dollhouses would be impressed by the detail, by the attention he gave to making a fully functioning house for dolls, even including moving windows, real electricity, and hand-carved side railings for the staircases.

It was only in the last year that Jack was able to develop this new creative gift, and he says with a degree of modesty that it is not difficult to do this after so much work in the construction business and having seen so many buildings go up. He simply tries to remember the details of homes he helped to build, and then, following from memory, re-creates them in a miniature size for miniature people.

Mass for terminal patients at St. Rose's Home

On beautiful days his wife takes him home in a wheelchair. They remember vividly a few years ago when he was given two weeks to live, coming here to St. Rose's, having no idea that he even had cancer. When I asked him what he thought he had, he said: "I thought I had gonorrhea in my leg, and my doctor told me that he treated me for gout." I asked him if the Sisters didn't tell him the truth and his response to that was, "The nuns said to my wife: 'If you want to tell him, go ahead; we won't tell him anything.'"

Jack told me it was taking him a long time to understand that he had cancer, and it was only about eight months ago that he realized what he had because "everybody who comes here has cancer, so why should I be an

Jack with his wife, Agnes, leaving St. Rose's for a weekend at home

Jack climbing stairs to his apartment

exception?" It was at this time that he started to do his wood-work, and, since he had all his experience in construction work, electrical work, plumbing and roofing, it gave him a new outlet and helped him to do something with his life. In his own words: "Now I get an idea for a house, I will gun it and get going on it."

Jack's own two children, his son and daughter, had married. He has never seen his grandchild. Since his son died two days before this visit to him, he plans to attend the funeral and hopes to see his granddaughter then. He believes it is a prejudice toward patients that makes adults leery about bringing children to places like this. When I asked him if he

Jack at home in kitchen with weekend medication

would recommend that grownups bring children of all ages to a home like this, he said with a great smile on his face: "The other hospital I detested, not only because they had given up hope on me and told me that I had two weeks to live, but because it was such a dreadful place that I would never bring anybody—neither grownups nor children—to such a hospital. Visitors would always remember it as a horrible place and would associate a terminal illness with a place like that. But here it is very different, and I would sure hope to have my children visit us here."

I asked him about the time when he's not working on his dollhouses or going home on short weekend visits. He told me with contentment and pride that one of his jobs at St. Rose's is watering the plants for those other patients who are bedridden. And so he is kept busy with a daily routine.

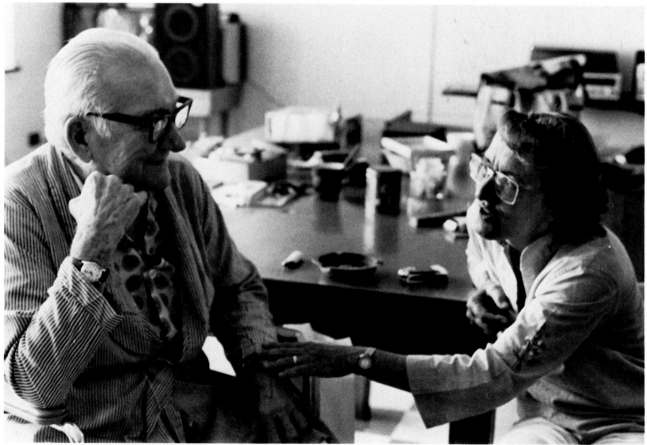

Jack during visit from Elisabeth Kübler-Ross

Jack, St. Rose's Home, watering flowers

One of the things that particularly impressed me at this home is that the men and women are in different units and do not eat together. While I was visiting during lunchtime in one of the rooms, it struck me at first as peculiar that each man ate at his own private table and did not share meals together in the same corner or at the same table. Jack very quickly explained this to me: "Yes, it is true, we eat alone at our own little tables. At first when I came here, I got involved with the patients, but many of them die very quickly and after a while I realized that I had to stay separate, at least sometimes, so I don't get too involved with them and, therefore, don't have to say good-bye continuously. Everybody here knows when somebody dies simply because the Sisters close the door. When somebody dies, I don't want to say good-bye. No, it is not that it is scary, or that I'm afraid. I hope there is an

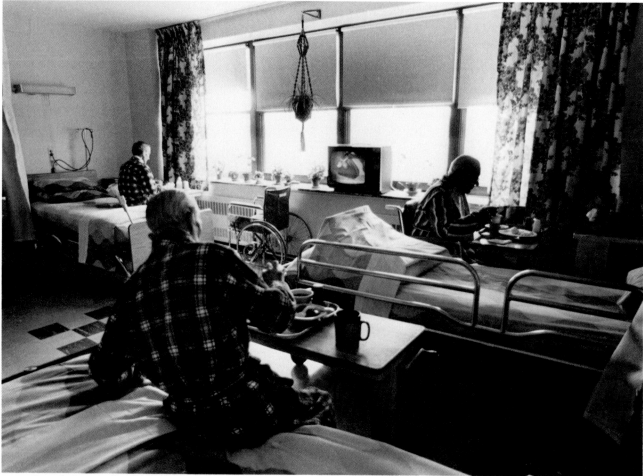

Lunchtime at St. Rose's

upstairs. I'm not that good. When I first came here, I wasn't
so good. But the Sisters are angels. They made a good man
out of me, and while giving me the medication, they prayed
with me and simply asked me if I would like to go to
confession and I did. Apparently I was ready for it. In the
other hospital I wouldn't want anybody to visit me. It was not
kept nice. It was most depressing. I wouldn't want to live or
die there. But here it is beautiful. When somebody dies, they
close the door and there is no sharing. Sometimes they come
and go within a few weeks and I don't want to get to know
them. I did only at the beginning. But I lost too many good
friends."

It is obvious that Jack has come a long way without being made to feel guilty. When he came, the Sisters accepted him for what he was. They have alcohol available, and Jack no longer misuses it. They have confession and prayers available, but they do not impose them on their patients. They have enough pain medication, and they are in the process of using the Brompton mixture for pain relief so that their patients will be able to sit up, to function, to be conscious to the end, and it is hoped to become as creative as Jack has become in the last two years. His creativity, like that of Beth's and Louise's, came to him as he started to live his life fully, something which is possible in a human, loving environment, and not possible in a sterile, mechanized hospital setting.

Elisabeth Kübler-Ross talking to Jack's wife, Agnes

Jack's wife visits with him several times a week at St. Rose's. She does not find this too difficult as she is able to take a taxicab. Neither room nor board nor the medical treatment nor the medication is an expense to them here. So they are able to afford the luxury of a taxi. I am sure that long after Jack dies, the dollhouses and the beautiful creations that Jack put together during his "bonus on life" will touch other people, little ones and big ones, and will be yet another demonstration that dying can be a nightmare in a depressing, sad hospital, but that it can also be a time of growth, creativity, and peace as it is at St. Rose's Homes across the country.

Jack, St. Rose's Home

2/Loving Care at Home

After five years at the University Hospital in Chicago, where I attended to dying patients and taught medical students, hospital chaplains, nurses, and social workers about the needs of dying patients—about their loneliness and about their ability to communicate if only they had a listening ear—it became clear that I had to leave. I had to leave so that others would have the courage to continue to serve and to listen to these patients, rather than to call on me for consultation. Yet only after I left the hospital did I realize that patients would continue to call, and that I was unable to visit them in hospitals where I no longer had hospital privileges.

   I started to reflect on the need for loving care, with adequate pain relief, in a positive and fear-free environment. Many of my patients and their families began to realize that they actually had a choice. Very few families had considered taking their patients home to die. Rather, it was the norm to send patients to the hospital when they were close to dying. Not only was this the norm throughout society, but it was almost expected; it implied that the family had done everything possible, that nobody was to blame, that the best specialists and the best equipment were nearby when their next of kin was close to the transition. It was a different thought and a different philosophy when they were confronted with our opposite approach, namely: Take them to the hospital only as long as appropriate treatment is available, as long as more chemotherapy and radiotherapy are needed, but take them home whenever treatment has failed to bring about positive results.

We naturally used the same approach with children who had brain tumors, after other treatments, including experimental drugs, had been used. There was a time when children themselves gave us the cues that they had had enough of all the shots, of all the bone marrow tests, of all the treatments. They wanted to go home. We were able to convey these wishes to the parents, who, often because of their own fears and their own anxieties, were unable to hear it. We showed it through the children's drawings, through their symbolic language communications. And many, many parents were able to hear the pleas of their little ones. Many a wife was able to take her husband home and many a husband was willing to take a wife home, as long as they had a support system, as long as they were able to call up somebody when they became frantic, anxious, or panicky because of some unexpected behavior or symptoms unfamiliar to the care-givers.

We were quite aware that very few physicians make house calls. And due to my extensive traveling, it was also clear that I could not be everywhere at one time, since my patients were located anywhere from San Francisco to New York. We simply challenged the families to consider the choice of taking their dying family members home, made ourselves available, and told them on which dates I would be able to contact them either by telephone or with a private house call. We would challenge them to do it; we confronted them with their own fears and we encouraged them to mobilize their courage to try it.

The beauty of these consultations was that they required very little time. Often within half an hour the families contemplated alternatives, became aware of the possibilities of taking a patient home. They began to appreciate the advantages of a familiar environment and also far less expensive care to their loved ones, the possibility of their physical, constant presence, and the most important fact that they—family and patient—actually had a choice.

After we discussed the matter with the terminally ill, many patients and families were willing to take a chance and discussed the matter with the treating physician. They often mobilized friends and neighbors to help them with the move back to their houses, with the changing experience, with the supply of an oxygen tent or a suction machine or a bed that is easily movable with a rubber ring. They found the help they needed to turn any living room into a comfortable sickroom.

The children in a household were perhaps most affected by this change, as many of the children had not seen their terminally ill Mommies and Daddies for weeks when they were away at hospitals. The joy was overwhelming when they realized that "Mommy is coming home once more." They were prepared for the fact that Mommy looked a little different, that Mommy was not able to do things for them anymore, or walk around. They were taught not to make too much noise, not to slam doors, and not to watch television unless they asked Mommy for permission first. But these little shortcomings and adjustments that the children had to make were more than compensated by the presence of their Mommy, who was still able to stroke their hair, who was still able to wave to them, to touch them and hold their hands and smile at them, able sometimes to shed a tear. Many children were held in Mommy's arms and again and again said, "Mommy, I'm so happy you're home." The most important thing, no matter how ill a parent is, is for a child to be near his or her mother or father, to have them physically close and not isolated and away at a hospital where children can never visit.

Children will even become cooks and servants and nursemaids. Little Rusty became a medical technician for his little sister, Jamie, and was able to take care of the suction machine and the oxygen tent. Contributing to the care of a little sister and also relieving the mother can give a child a tremendous sense of achievement. It became important to emphasize this to families and to make them realize that one person alone can never take care of a terminally ill patient, that it takes a minimum of two people in order for life to continue as naturally and as normally as possible.

The wife of a terminally ill man was encouraged to continue to go to the hairdresser once a week if she did that before the illness. A man was encouraged to go bowling with his friends once a week if that's what he did prior to his wife's illness. It is important that family members continue to live, that they do not wean themselves from all other relationships, since the loss would be enormous and that would make the restarting (after a death had occurred) far more difficult. Children should be allowed to bring friends home, even though they may have to play quietly in another room. We have encouraged them to talk with the patients, whether they are siblings, parents, or grandparents, about anything they want to talk about, including the impending death or funeral arrangements. They have discussed these things with their dying Mommies and Daddies, with their brothers and sisters, and sometimes even with grandmas and grandpas, who seemed to be more reluctant to talk about them.

Children often finish the unfinished business for parents. Such a situation occurred in the house of a terminally ill mother. Her husband was no longer able to tolerate the situation and in an expression of impotent rage and anguish, he hollered at her that he was sorry he had ever married her, that he would put the children into foster homes and that he would think about it twice before he married again. He left his 28-year-old wife in tears and agony in the hospital, totally despondent and feeling unable to do anything for her children, one and five years old. A girl friend who visited her became aware of this disaster, pleaded with the physician to discharge this young dying woman, and called me for a consultation. I prepared the husband to take his young wife home in order to finish their unfinished business. He was more than appreciative, and he cooperated. I then sat with the one-year-old and the five-year-old at the kitchen table asking the five-year-old to draw a picture and to tell me all about Mommy's illness and her dying.

On the second evening after the patient's return home, I made another house call and we decided also to invite the patient's parents, who had a bad relationship with their daughter and who had their own private problems not related to their young daughter's impending death. The mother was a hypochondriac and the father had been an alcoholic for 15 years, almost incommunicable with wife and daughter and rejected by the family, all of whom were alienated from him. Their idea was that they were too "weak" and unable to stand the stress of watching their daughter's death. I was of a different opinion. I believed that they had the right to be with their one and only daughter, and that it might give them the strength to overcome their own weaknesses.

As it turned out, we were able to put the patient under the living room window in a comfortable bed. I was sitting with the one-year-old and the five-year-old on my lap in front of her, her husband on my left, and her mother on my right. Automatically and without thinking, her mother reached out and put her arm over her husband's shoulder. He was very touched and moved by this unexpected closeness; he reached out to his daughter, who was holding her husband's hand, and without planning or rehearsing anything, we suddenly became a circle of human beings surrounding this young woman at the time of her premature but beautiful and peaceful death.

A few hours before her death, she opened her eyes and looked smiling at her family and at us holding her children on our lap. It was at this moment that the five-year-old started to verbalize all the unspoken words that the grownups were unable to share. She looked at her Mommy and then at me and said suddenly, "Dr. Kübler-Ross, do you think it's all right if I pray to God tonight that he can take my Mommy?"

I told her it would be all right, that God would understand and listen to her prayers. After a moment of thought she turned around again and said, "I hope He doesn't mind if I add another prayer after that and tell Him to send her back again." I told her that she could say anything that she wanted to God, that He would hear and understand, but that she could be sure that she would see her Mommy again. But she also had to understand that in the place where Mommy was going time was very different from our time, and though she would certainly see her Mommy again, it would not be tomorrow or the day after tomorrow. After a few moments of reflection, this little girl looked again at Mommy and then said, "If this Mommy dies, does that mean that I'm going to get a foster mother?"

Silently the young mother touched her husband's hand, expressing her concern about their short and painful marriage to one another and encouraging him to go ahead and marry another woman if he should find one who truly loved him and who could bring him more happiness than they had in their short marriage together. By then, they all had tears in their eyes. The five-year-old continued, undisturbed by the turmoil of the grownups. She asked, "If all my Mommies die, who's going to cook for me?"

I laughed and told her that I had a big kitchen and if all her Mommies should die, which was highly improbable, she could always move into my house and I would always love to cook for her. She put her warm, cuddly arms around me and gave me a big hug. A little while later we asked her to kiss her Mommy goodnight and we tucked the two children into bed shortly before ten o'clock. A neighbor brought me home an hour later, and shortly before midnight I received a telephone call that the young mother had died peacefully in her sleep. Not only were we able to prevent a guilt-ridden, grief-stricken widower who would have had a hard time starting a new life and eventually getting remarried, but we were able to help two young children to be present at one of the most important moments in life, namely at the time of their mother's transition, shared with three generations.

With her favorite music playing, with candlelight on the table, with the children near, and with flowers next to her picked by her own children, she died a very different kind of death than had she stayed in the hospital. Those children will never associate death with loneliness, isolation, playing games, and deceit. They will remember it as a time of togetherness with their parents, grandparents, and friends who cared and were able to acknowledge their own anxieties and their own fears, and together were able to overcome them.

After having witnessed a few deaths like this in a home, it became very clear that every person has such an opportunity. Home care rather than a hospital or a nursing home is always possible when there is a support system available. And it requires very little time on our part to be the facilitator and the catalyst of such a constructive, positive choice.

Patient outdoors at Wisconsin Hospice

3/Hospice:
Patients Who Live Until They Die

There are a few people who have no families. There are a few cancers that cause a great discomfort and smell. There are old people who simply do not have the strength to care for a mate. And for all those people, a hospice is the answer. The word hospice hundreds of years ago referred to a place up in the mountains in Switzerland where the monks took care of the people who traversed the mountain passes. These were the same monks who became famous for the raising and training of the St. Bernard dogs, who in turn became famous for digging the victims out of the avalanches. The Hospice of St. Bernard had always taken care of needy people, injured or tired travelers, and accident victims. Later on hospices started up in England for the care of dying patients. The best known in Great Britain is the hospice in Sydenham, where the original Brompton mixture was used and where the average stay of terminally ill patients is sixteen days prior to death. In the United States, the Hospice of New Haven in Connecticut was the first one that opened its doors to a home care program in order to give people the total patient care that is necessary when cure, active treatment, and prolongation of life are no longer the goal. Since the opening of the Hospice in New Haven, we have been able to facilitate and encourage 55 other places in the United States to develop a hospice, and it is a rare state that does not have such a facility at least in the planning stages.

The Home Care Unit at the New Haven Hospice

A participant in one of my one-week workshops presented me with a Christmas gift of a hospice, the first in Wisconsin. He used a building which had existed for many decades as a psychiatric hospital and was no longer in use. Rather than spend fortunes in building new facilities, he made use of the existing structure, which is on the premises of a beautiful park surrounded by meadows, trees, and flowers. He and his workers were able to start a unit where patients find a home, love, and total patient care. There are many hospices now across the United States, and it is hoped that for those few people who do not have a family support system to take care of their final days in their own homes, there will always be a hospice available to them. There they will be helped to live until they die: they will not have to spend their energy, their financial resources, and their hopes on the prolongation of life; they will not be surrounded with dehumanizing machines, technology, and efficient staffs, who unfortunately will never have enough time simply to sit and hold a hand or listen to a patient reflecting on his or her life

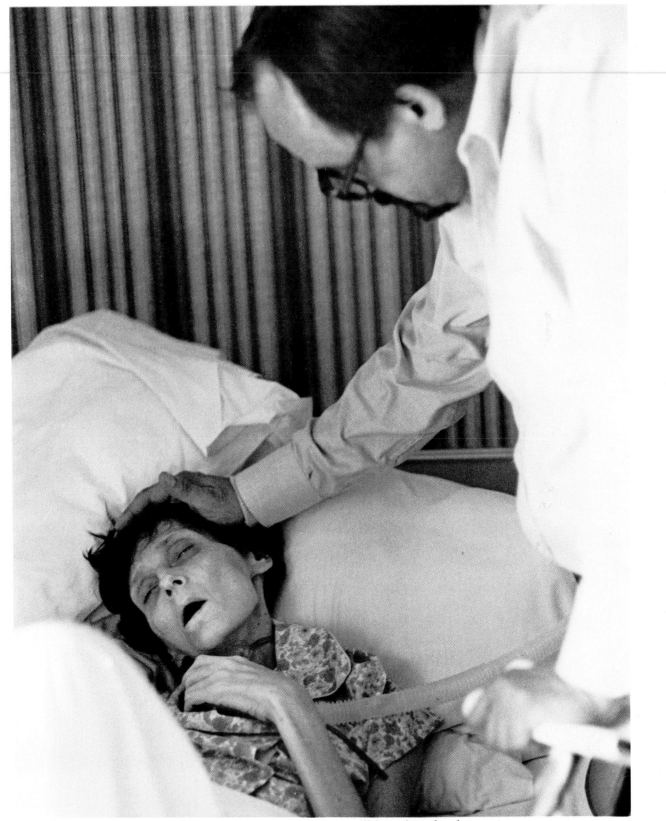

"The two promises we make to our patients are: one, we will keep them free from pain; two, they will not die alone," Rev. Michael Stolpman, Director, Wisconsin Hospice

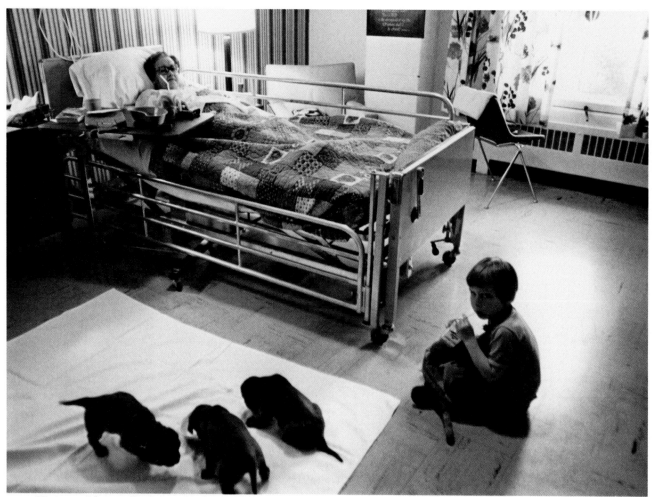

Visitor with puppies in patient's room at Wisconsin Hospice

without a page calling them away, a supervisor reprimanding them, or an emergency calling them "back to duty."

There are few, if any, nursing homes in this country that try to create programs to help people live until they die or try to enhance their clients' ability to share and to give and to be creative. Almost all nursing homes in the United States are geared to the clients' receiving services—but no patient, man or woman, will ever get a sense of pride, of self-respect, or of dignity, if all that is being offered is basic services. Another important issue is that hospices cost a fraction of what hospital care costs, and it is not right that people at the end of their life, when they have enough problems to contend with, also have to be burdened with the tremendous, out-of proportion medical and hospital care costs.

Some years ago I had the opportunity of visiting the St. Rose's Home in Fall River, Massachusetts, a branch of the St. Rose's Home in New York City where our friend Jack is. I was most impressed that there was such a hospital already in existence that very few people knew of. It was a private old mansion that was turned into a hospice for indigent, terminally ill patients, run by Dominican Sisters in the most loving, caring manner that I have ever witnessed in this country. In spite of the fact that I was an unexpected visitor arriving at 9:00 P.M., the Sisters showed me around and gave me permission to talk to any patient or staff member during my brief and unforgettable visit.

There was a beautiful sun porch full of flowers. The patients looked well-kept and cared for, and the Sisters emphasized that they were all supported by private funds and

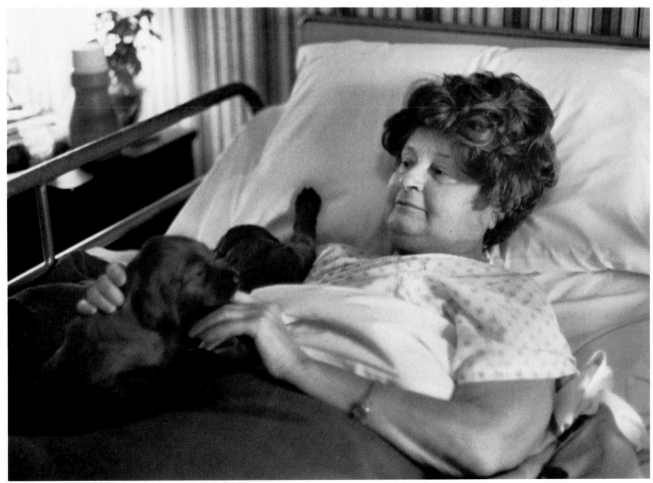

Patient with puppies at Wisconsin Hospice

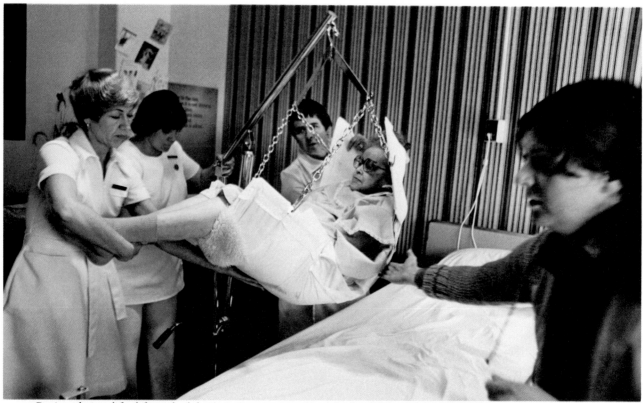

Patient being lifted from bed for hairdressing appointment at Wisconsin Hospice

that they took only people who were unable to get any
financial support to accommodate them in some of the
expensive hospitals. All services were free to these patients
and the staff made sure that they had all their needs met. It
sounded so remarkable that I was most skeptical, and after all
the visitors left, I sneaked back into one of the rooms of the
patients and asked the first woman in the first bed, "What is
it really like here?" With a beaming face she looked at me and
said, "There is no better place on earth to live," with the
emphasis on the living.

It is noteworthy that the seven St. Rose's homes in the
United States have received very little publicity though they
are a blessing to those who can ill afford the present-day
expensive hospitalizations in the face of a long-term illness.
All these patients are taken care of with tender, loving care
and without any expense to them or their families, and
without any expectations for rewards in any material sense.
The rewards that the St. Rose's staff receives come in the
form of love, appreciation, and gratitude—and, I'm sure, with

many blessings for the unconventional love that they give their patients. Anyone who looks at the pictures of the woman or the man in the St. Rose's Home in New York City will see the pride, dignity, and peace in their faces and will know that there is a place like this in this country that is worth our support and our prayers.

It is hoped that with more hospices and home care facilities, our next generation of children will never again have to see a sign, "No Children Under Age 14 Allowed in the Hospital." It is hoped that all the children of our next generation will be permitted to face the realities of life. It is hoped that we will not "protect" them as a reflection of our own fears and our

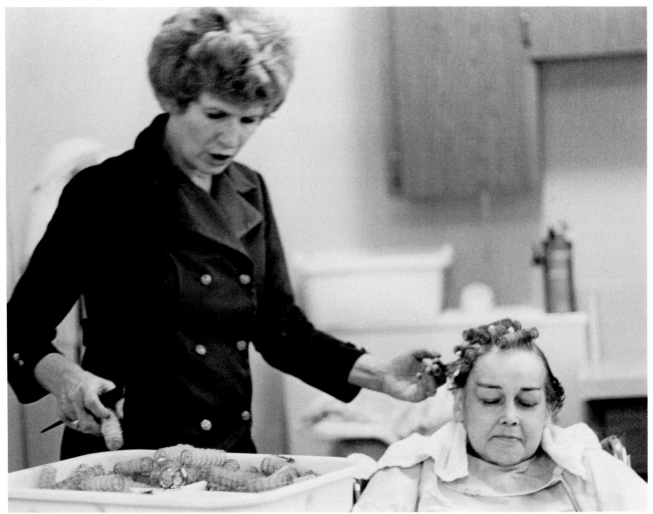

Patient at hairdresser, Wisconsin Hospice

own anxieties! It is hoped that we adults are beginning to have the courage to realize that it is our fear that we project onto the next generation. Once we have courage enough, we can acknowledge honestly that there are problems, and we can solve them if we have someone who cares and who facilitates the expression of our fears and guilts and unfinished business. If we can do this, we can empty our pool of repressed negativity and start living fully and more harmoniously.

Children who have been exposed to these kinds of experiences—in a safe, secure, and loving environment—will then raise another generation of children who will, most likely, not even comprehend that we had to write books on death and dying and had to start special institutions for the

Patient at St. Rose's Home, New York

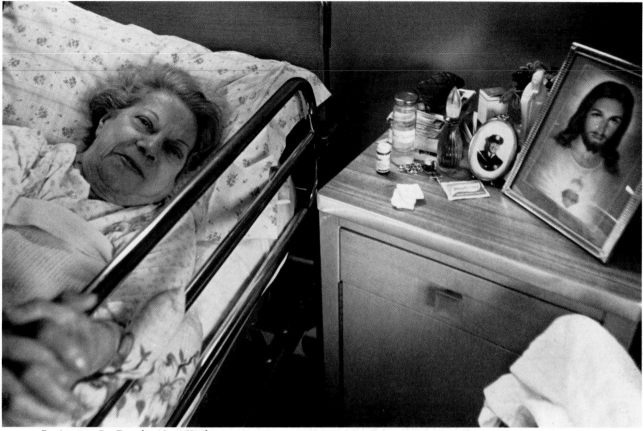
Patient at St. Rose's, New York

dying patients; they will not understand why there was this
overwhelming fear of death, which, for so long covered up the
fear of living.

We appreciate the care and love that is given to our patients
in the hospices across the country. We appreciate the
willingness of staff members to share their work in pictures
and words with the readers of this book. It is always a mutual
benefit. We have helped them to get off their feet. We have
tried to make society aware of the needs of dying patients.
And they have been able to hear us and have supplied us with
facilities that are open to those who cannot go home. One day
some of us will need a place, and by then the hospices will
have sprung up all over the country. There will be at least one
in every state—as there will be a Shanti Nilaya, our own
Growth and Healing Center, in every state of this country—so
that we do not have to wait until we are dying but will be

Patient at St. Rose's, New York

able to get in touch with our unfinished business, with our fears, guilts, and shames, before we have a terminal illness, so we can live at our fullest. And so we will be ready even if death should come in a sudden and unexpected way.

Shanti Nilaya means "The final home of peace." There will be many final homes of peace, but we cannot find peace if we are afraid of the windstorms of life. We cannot give peace to our children if we protect them like greenhouse plants. The children who will have peace are those who have had parents who knew what unconditional love meant, who have had parents who did not shield them from the first steps away from home. These children will have parents who did not hold them back when they entered the first school bus to go to the first frightening day at school—parents who knew how to put training wheels on a tricycle but were also willing to take those training wheels off when the child was ready to ride without them.

Patient at St. Rose's, New York

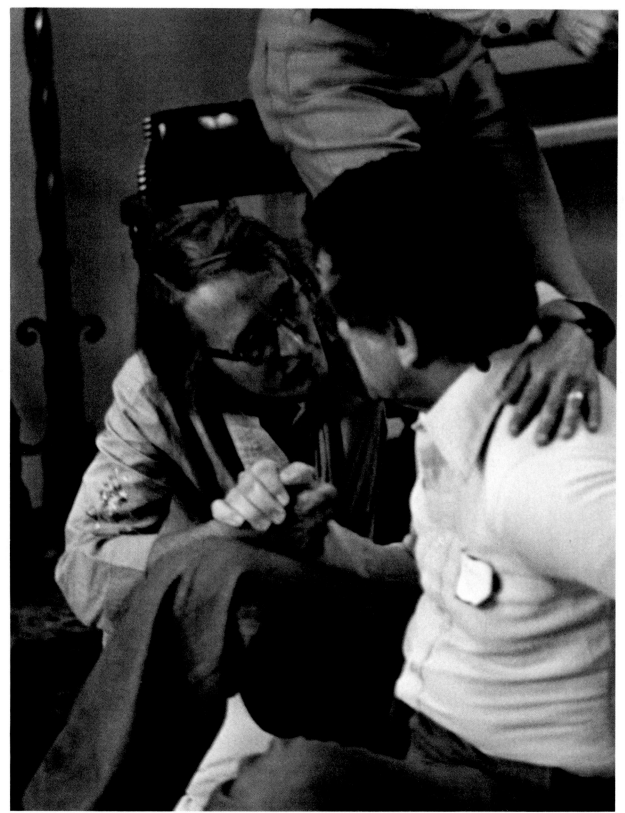

Elisabeth Kübler-Ross with workshop participant, Appleton, Wisconsin

4/Teaching About Life, Death, and Transition: *Shanti Nilaya*

How do we train hospital staff and lay people, family members of dying patients and those at the beginning of a terminal illness, when they are still able to be mobile, for a life of creativity in the face of impending death?

One of the tools that we use is our one-week workshops on life, death, and transition which we give across the country to anyone from age 16 to 89 who is willing to spend five days at a retreat, usually a site away from a large city and one that is not used by any other group or organization. The participants range from the medical directors and physicians to engineers, social workers, nurses, clergy, students, housewives, yoga teachers, philosophers, and poets. They usually include parents of dying children, or those whose children have been murdered. They always include terminally ill patients of all ages except young children. There are healthy people whose lives have been touched by an experience of death or tragedy, people who are willing to take a look at their own values and to reevaluate the direction in which they are going, whether they are aware of the shortness of their life or not. Lay people and professionals, young and old, believers and agnostics, share this experience together and emerge from it changed.

The purpose of these workshops is to share with a group of 70 people everything we have learned from the dying patient who has been our teacher for the last twelve years. We

Elisabeth Kübler-Ross conducting workshop at Appleton, Wisconsin

allow the participants to share their own griefs, search for their own unfinished business, for their own fears and guilts, and we help them to relive and externalize their negative feelings in order to find peace and to do away with the drain of energy required to repress all these negative feelings. We help them to free themselves of guilt and fear, and we try to teach them unconditional love and service to their fellowman so that they can return to their homes, schools, hospitals, or places of work and do those things that our dying patients learn to do in the final days of their physical life—things that regrettably no one helped them accomplish earlier so that they would have been able to say, "I have truly lived."

The workshops are held throughout the country and, naturally, vary a great deal from place to place, depending almost exclusively on how much the participants are willing to share and contribute. A simple technique of using a piece of rubber hose to beat a mattress facilitates the expression of pain, rage, and impotence, and triggers off similar feelings in those who listen to the courageous sharing. In order to make this experience available to more people, some of whom have had to be put on as much as a two-year waiting list for a workshop, we searched for a permanent place where people of

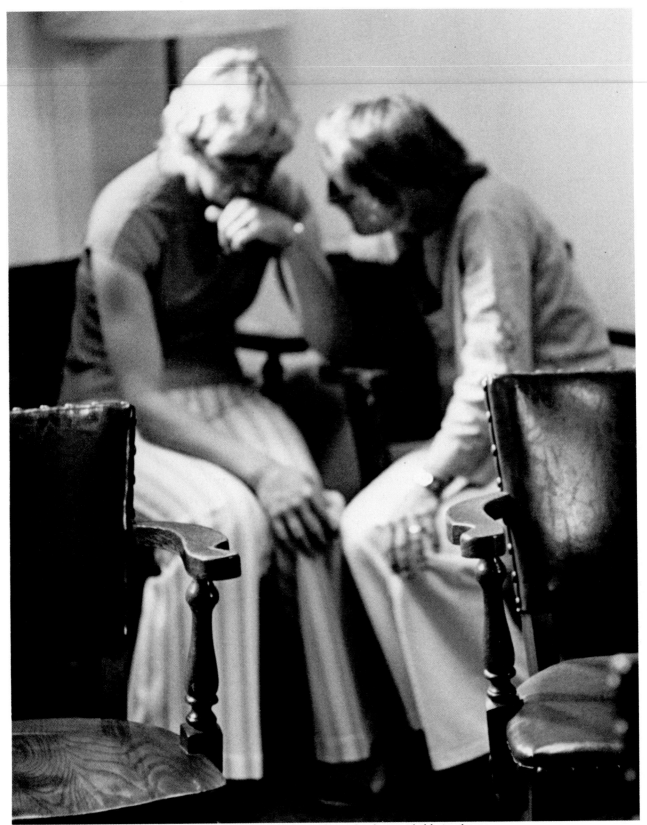

Elisabeth Kübler-Ross talking at workshop with mother who lost a child, Appleton, Wisconsin

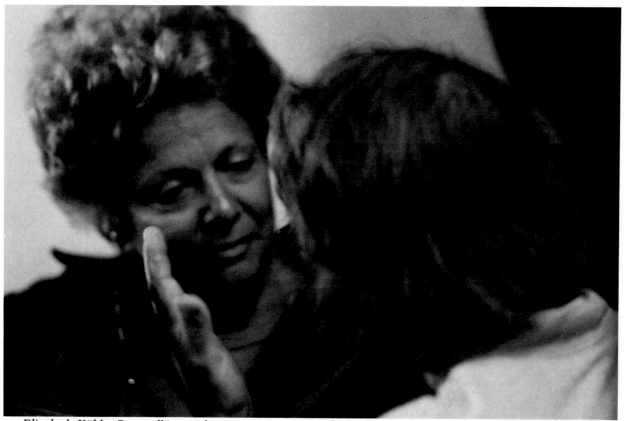

Elisabeth Kübler-Ross talking with cancer patient at Appleton, Wisconsin, workshop

all ages, backgrounds, creeds, and financial resources would be able to come and receive this kind of help.

In November of 1977 we were able to open our own growth and healing center, Shanti Nilaya, words which mean a Final Home of Peace. It is located above Escondido in California, in a private place surrounded by mountains. Eventually it will serve as our permanent retreat where we have planned special facilities for quadriplegics, for terminally ill children, for youngsters with problems and where adults of all ages and backgrounds will be able to come and participate in workshops to learn how to live until they die.

Shanti Nilaya will, we hope, be a place of peace for those who seek answers about the meaning and purpose of life and death, of suffering and pain, not only of the physical body, but of the whole person. It is our dream that we will be able to start building other Shanti Nilayas soon and that in the next ten years we will be able to erect a Shanti Nilaya in every state of the United States and abroad—a place not for

Cancer patient at workshop, Shanti Nilaya

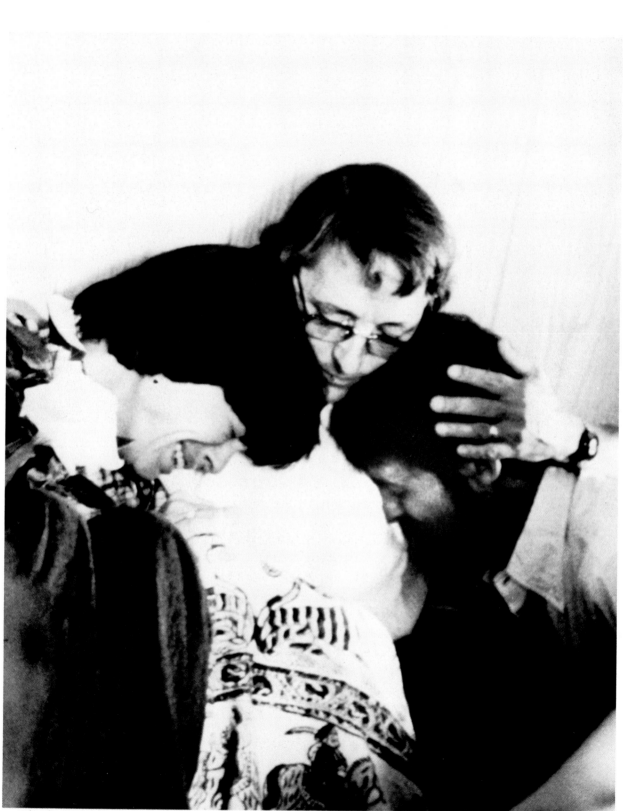

Elisabeth Kübler-Ross and Linda at Shanti Nilaya workshop. Dr. Kübler-Ross presented a lily to Linda to mark the day that would have been Jamie's sixth birthday.

Session with rubber hose, Shanti Nilaya

the dying but for all those who have the courage to face their own fears and who, instead of avoiding them or repressing them, will be willing to move toward them and leave them behind.

What we try to teach at Shanti Nilaya, and in our workshops, is perhaps best described in our first Shanti Nilaya calendar where we describe the meaning of true love. It is the teachings of our own teachers and simply states: "To love means not to impose your own powers on your fellowman but offer him your help. And if he refuses it, to be proud that he can do it on his own strength. To love means to live without fear and anxieties about tomorrow. To love means never to be afraid of the windstorms of life: Should you shield the canyons from the windstorms you would never see the true beauty of their carvings.

I hope that this book encourages people to expose themselves to these windstorms, so that at the end of their own days, they will be proud to look in the mirror and be pleased with the carvings of their own canyon.

Elisabeth Kübler-Ross, Shanti Nilaya

INDEX